MU00614928

Prais

YOUR REJECTION, GOD'S PROTECTION

"Your Rejection, God's Protection: A Unique Biblical Approach to Understanding Rejection is a real-life experience written with rare transparency that meticulously details the anguish of rejection. Among its resounding themes are that the path to destiny involves roads of rejection, that rejection is not exclusive to color, wealth nor status, and that the Word of God is the inimitable source for wholeness in and through and after experiencing rejection. Cheryl and Micah Chavers exhibit a heart to help others while facing their own rejection. They hold to their faith with doors closing in their faces, trusting their God who is orchestrating the process. They refuse to accept the lie that they have been rejected by God."

> —**Bishop Lewis L. Stokes, Vice Presiding Bishop,**
> **United Church of Jesus Christ (Apostolic) and**
> **Elder Brenda M. Stokes, Assistant Pastor,**
> **United Family Worship Center**

"This little gem is sure to lift your spirits and expand your perspective on rejection and its sequelae. Good medicine for your soul, not only when you are feeling down but essential reading in preparation for those painful and unpleasant experiences that will undoubtedly come your way. Recounting their personal experience with rejection and with vignettes of select biblical characters, the authors captivate the reader with their thoughtful and creative approach. A reassuring theme is that God loves us so much, that in His omniscience He sometimes allows personal rejection to occur, if it means protecting us from something much worse."

> —**Wayne L. Greaves, Physician**

"The silent cries of rejection has been heard from God's people and He has sent a deliverer. This book provides insight, understanding and eventual deliverance. As you read this book, I believe if your heart is open and honest with yourself, the Holy Spirit can heal you. This book reminds us that we are surrounded by such a great cloud of witnesses, past and present. Therefore, we also can overcome the slights of rejection. In reading through the passages, there were areas where I needed to repent for giving up and ask God to help me believe that He still has plans for me."

—Starlene L. Aydlett, Professional School Counselor

"Gives a whole new perspective on 'rejection' with sound biblically based references to God's protection. This is a must read for believers challenged with adversity. The testimonies provided throughout this 5 chapter book give credence to the fact that we as believers will not be immune to adversity, but if we look at the push back, rejection or delay as possibly a sign from He who is able to do exceedingly and abundantly more than we can ask or think. This book is a great tool to help us through the process of WAITING. Micah and Cheryl Chavers thank you for being obedient and the messenger of a good word in due season."

—Shannon Sims, News TV Anchor

"*Your Rejection, God's Protection* is absolutely superb. It is both inspirational and informational with very practical, love-filled and prayerfully rich to help a broad spectrum of audiences. A must read for anyone looking to enrich their whole-being . . . What a blessing!!!"

—Elisa Sharps, ND, Executive Director of IIOM

"The power of the individual story—Jesus employed it in His use of parables. Cheryl Osbourne Chavers and Micah Chavers have created this instructive and insightful book based on the individual stories of Biblical characters. How amazing and comforting it is to know that the rejections, disappointments, and slights we experience in life are the fodder for God's perfect creative expression. These stories, as retold through the eyes of the authors, show us and remind us to have faith and to believe!"

—Sedora Jefferson, Attorney at Law

"*Your Rejection, God's Protection! A Unique Biblical Approach to Understanding Adversity,* is eloquently written with God's truths that will speak to your heart and draw you into deeper relationship with our Heavenly Father. The examples used from God's chosen vessels are brought alive in this book and remind us that it's not over until it's over. Cheryl and Micah, thank you for your perseverance and obedience to the Lord's vision for this book!"

—Joi Harris, Licensed Clinical Social Worker

Your Rejection, God's Protection:
A Unique Biblical Approach to
Understanding Adversity!

by Cheryl Osbourne Chavers & Micah Chavers

© Copyright 2017 Cheryl Osbourne Chavers & Micah Chavers

ISBN 978-1-63393-511-2

Published by

◤ köehlerbooks™

210 60th Street
Virginia Beach, VA 23451
800-435-4811
www.koehlerbooks.com

Your Rejection, God's Protection

A Unique Biblical Approach to Understanding Adversity!

CHERYL OSBOURNE CHAVERS
& MICAH CHAVERS

VIRGINIA BEACH
CAPE CHARLES

CONTENTS

ACKNOWLEDGMENTS

Heavenly Father,

Thank you for this incredible journey with You! We marvel at the keen insights you have provided in this book and are grateful to be used as vessels to enlighten your people. May your name be praised always!

A special thank you:

To Maylin, our lovely daughter, who is such a blessing and a delight. Thank you for your contribution and support along the way.

To our nurturing and loving parents, H. Augustus and Gladys Osbourne, Ronald and Gillian Chavers, and our grandmother, Susie Jefferson, thank you for your support and love.

To our wonderful siblings, Elisa, Ember, Ian, and Johnni, and our amazing and supportive family members, we love and appreciate you.

To the spiritually uplifting congregations who have helped to nurture the seeds God planted in our lives—Calvary Seventh-day Adventist Church (Newport News, Virginia); Mercy Seat Baptist Church (Hampton, Virginia); Westmount Seventh-day Adventist Church (Montreal, Canada).

To spiritual mentors and friends who provided guidance along our journey—Pastor Ronald and Dena Reeves; Pastor Trevor and Carleen Kinlock; Pastor T. DuWayne and Theresa Privette; Professor Gregory S. Mims; Martha Askew; Elders Andrew and Minnie McNeil; Elder Jeffery Thomas; Rolston and Kristal Audain; Randy and Natoya Nelson; Jerry Ray Howard II and Dr. Sylvette LaTouche Howard.

To all our friends who shared their testimonies and have given such tremendous support in this endeavor, we are blessed because of your exceptional friendship. Thank you!

FOREWORD

Fill in the blanks: When life gives you lemons, you make . . . that's right, lemonade! However, what happens when life gives you the sour seeds of the lemon in the form of disappointment, and more importantly, feelings of sheer rejection? Truly, what do you do? You become motivated, determined, and truly creative, and not only do you figure out a way to make something refreshing that is even better than lemonade, but you make enough to share with everyone! That makes absolutely no sense . . . at all!

To the naked eye, this would be true, but if I were to tell you that this is the reason why I appreciate the principles set forth in this book, you will start to understand. This book is a "long time coming," and I am truly excited about the lives that it will not only touch but also empower and bless. I pray that as you read through the pages of this book, you will be inspired, changed, and transformed.

—Dr. Sylvette A. La Touche-Howard, PhD, NCC, CHES

PREFACE

Writing this book has been a long journey that has taken many years to complete. In doing so we were reminded that, in order to tell others about hope after rejection, we too would have to experience the anguish that comes with rejection. How could we possibly encourage others if we didn't experience it firsthand? In our attempt to publish this book we were met with rejection over and over again. This made us apply the principles we so passionately wrote about to our very own lives. Based on these experiences, we find the strategies outlined in the book to be reliable. Here is our publishing rejection story.

In our quest to get this book published we submitted the manuscript to several publishers with the hope that they would catch the vision and be willing to take on our project. Unfortunately, each publisher stated that it was a great idea but that they would not be able to publish our book. Needless to say, we were very disappointed, but then we looked at each other and asked ourselves this: How could we possibly be upset about rejection when we were writing a book to help people learn how to deal with rejection? We could not be hypocritical!

So, we put into practice the principles the Lord allowed us to write about in the book. We *refocused* on the task at hand, diligently searching for a publisher that would publish our book. A friend of ours recently published her book and we decided to call her and ask about her publishing experience. We spoke for a while and she shared her positive experience with a renowned publishing firm. We decided to send them our manuscript to see if they would be interested. Shortly thereafter, we received a phone call from one of their acquisition editors, who said he read our manuscript and would like to have an interview with us to discuss things further.

Our conversation went very well, and we felt confident that they understood the concept and would be a good fit to publish the book. We signed the contract and began the work of completing the rest of the book. Life got busy and other priorities took place over writing, but from time to time we would feel the prompting of the Holy Spirit to finish up this divine assignment. We *repented* for procrastinating and asked the Lord's forgiveness for casting aside the divine assignment given to us. In obedience, we completed the book and felt a sense of relief when we finished writing the very last chapter and sent it off to our editor for review. While the editing process was underway, the graphic designer sent us some book cover designs to review. This step really got us excited as we narrowed down what we wanted the book cover to look like.

Just as we were making progress and thinking that the project would be finished, the publishing process halted. We tried to reach out to our editor and graphic designer and got no response. Phone calls and emails went unanswered for weeks, and our attempt to reach anyone at the company was to no avail. Here we were writing a book about rejection and we were experiencing rejection by our very own publisher!

Finally, we received an email from the firm, but it was not the news we were hoping to hear. The company was suspending operations, with a request for all clients to complete a contract release form and the forfeiture of any investment in the project. Even more astonishing, we read news reports about the company being sued by companies that they owed money to, and we were shocked when we saw reports of the arrests of the company's leadership for embezzlement, extortion, and racketeering. We were heartbroken and bitterly disappointed with the realization that our investment, hopes, and dreams for this book were gone.

But once again, the Lord reminded us about the principles in the book, and we halfheartedly decided to put them into practice and regroup. While still smarting from the rejection, the Lord strategically presented us with another opportunity. One day, while reading a local online newspaper, our attention was grabbed by a feature article on a book publishing firm that was locally based. The article detailed that the company worked on the autobiography of a nationally known restauranteur and businessman. It appeared that, even though they were considered a small firm, their reputation for excellence in publishing was quite distinguished.

We diligently researched the company and noticed that they were located in a neighboring city, close to where we lived, and the information on their website piqued our interest. We prayed about it and then submitted our manuscript. Immediately, we were contacted by an acquisitions editor, and we shared our sad tale about being rejected by our publisher and the search for a new one. A face to face meeting with the president was set up, and we felt immediately that we were in the right place as we were introduced to staff members. We learned more from the president about the publishing world in one sitting than we did in the years we worked with the now defunct publishing company.

The Lord answered our prayer and we *rejoiced* as we decided to partner together in publishing this book. It truly has been a professional and remarkable experience and we are grateful for their guidance. We realize now that *our rejection* was *God's protection*, because if we had finished publishing with the other firm, our book would've been tied up in litigation for years, quite possibly never having the opportunity to be released. Although it was difficult to go through at the time, we *recall* this experience to encourage others to forge ahead in the midst of adversity, because if the Lord could bring us through, then surely He can do the same for you!

May God bless you,

Cheryl & Micah

INTRODUCTION
GOD'S PERFECT TIMING

I WAS BURNT OUT, had nothing left to give, and I felt like imploding. My nerves were on edge, I desperately needed a change, and I wanted a way out! I had been employed as a social worker for several years, helping to stabilize families who were in crisis, and preventing children from being separated from their parents and placed in the custody of the State. With *unlimited* problems and limited resources to help these families, I found myself in a Band-Aid crisis state. No sooner did one issue get resolved than another popped up. While trying to fix one problem after the other, I prayed to God that something tragic wouldn't happen to these children on my watch.

Feelings of hopelessness permeated my head while I struggled to find a work balance. I would even wake up in the middle of the night to check my work voicemail to make sure that there were no messages from clients in distress. My greatest fear was that I would have a major crisis waiting for me the next morning when I got to work. In my mind, I didn't feel equipped to help families, effect positive change, and make a genuine difference in the lives of my clients. Sometimes, the very families I was trying to help would reject my presence in their home, yelling at me, slamming the door in my face or cursing at me on the phone. Now I was the one feeling bruised, abused, busted, and disgusted. With my mindset, it felt like I was doing an injustice serving families when I felt so overwhelmed, burnt out, and incompetent.

I prayed about it and felt like it was time for me to move on and look for another job. So, I started the process, spruced up my resume, and began applying for different jobs in the field of social work. Every day, I eagerly waited for a change, but nothing happened! Every job interview I went on resulted in me being rejected. I cried out to the Lord, please make a way, and open a door for me to escape this burden. My nerves were frayed and I was desperate. I felt as though I couldn't continue to juggle my entire caseload without dropping the ball and negatively impacting the families that I served. Despite my prayers, perseverance, and continued job interviews, every phone call I received from a prospective employer told me that I had all the skills and qualifications, but they had found another candidate who was a better fit for the position. I continued to feel rejected, asking the Lord why he didn't hear my desperate pleas and provide a way of escape for me to get out of this job!

Finally, after months of searching, applying, and interviewing, I got my breakthrough. The Lord answered my prayers and I was offered a new position! To my surprise, it was a newly created position, within the same agency I worked for. The job had everything I was looking for, including more career benefits than I had before. I was offered a promotion to a senior level position with a significant pay raise, and I would be instrumental in establishing new engagement techniques with a creative approach to working with families.

With tears in my eyes, I thanked and praised the Lord for answering my prayers. With this abundant blessing bestowed on me, the Lord revealed Himself to me in a powerful way. Looking back on this situation, the Lord's timing was clearly evident, and I began to see the rejection I had initially encountered in a new light. Every position I was denied, there was a reason for it. The rejection I experienced was not really rejection, but God's *protection*! All those times that I was being rejected by prospective employers, God was protecting me. In His infinite wisdom, the Lord knew that the other positions I applied for would have only left me more stressed and burnt out, than in my previous position.

At the time, I wasn't able to wrap my mind around this concept because my eyes were blinded with the need for an immediate resolution. All I was thinking about was "woe is me" and how burnt out I was. I couldn't see God preparing a way for me and setting the platform for a job that was better than I ever imagined.

It wasn't until after I got the position that I was able to place things in perspective. I saw the Lord as a masterful chess player, vigilantly observing His children. He strategically preserves, intently holds, plans, and skillfully maneuvers His children to the right place at the right time until victory is won. However, sometimes in our haste and desire to see things happen right away, we begin to doubt God and His limitless possibilities. We often negate what the Lord has in store for us, when the word of God clearly states, "For I know the plans I have for you, [. . .] plans to prosper you and not to harm you, plans to give you hope and a future."[1] So even when it seems like nothing is working according to plan, know the Lord has a divine assignment for your life, one that will ultimately bless you.

* * *

Rejection is to be expected

When you think of the word rejection, it definitely does not conjure up warm and fuzzy feelings. Rejection is a word that makes people feel uncomfortable. It's hard to imagine anyone who willingly wants to experience the pain that comes with being rejected. One way *not* to win friends and influence people is to go into a crowded room and ask if anyone wants to hear how many times you've been rejected in life. It's almost guaranteed that you'll experience

---

1   Jer. 29:11 New International Version

awkward glances and the silent treatment as people quickly try to get away from you and leave the room.

Being rejected can be a horrible experience. It is an uncomfortable topic that no one likes to talk about because it brings up painful moments in life when things did not go according to plan. Bringing up the topic of rejection and talking about it is like digging into a wound that has yet to heal. There are many people who can't even make it through the day because of rejection they experienced as a child that transfixed and changed the course of their entire life. As crippling as it can be, one certainty is that rejection is inescapable, and it has the ability to follow you wherever you go, whether it's at home, work, in the community, and even in places of worship.

* * *

Home

The lyrics of a lovely Christian song are "If home is truly where the heart is, then home must be a place we all can share."[2] While the sentiments of this song may ring true for some, for others home is anything but that! Home is supposed to be a place of solace and refuge shielding you from the ills of the world, enveloping you in its warm embrace.

What happens when your home is a place where you are scorned, abused, and even rejected? For example, what happens when the very place a father is supposed to be the king of his castle is the same place where he is treated like an outcast? Or what about the home where mom, the nurturing parent, favors one child while rejecting and belittling the other? What about the wrath of siblings, readily pouncing and ejecting you from their inner circle?

The Bible chronicles a multitude of stories that depict the sad renderings of familial rejection. Two of these examples are the story

---

2   Patty, Sandi. "Love Will Be Our Home." *Make His Praise Glorious.* Word Entertainment, 1988.

of David and his siblings, who characterized him as a nuisance,[3] and the even more horrid tale of David's daughter, Tamar, who was brutally attacked by her own step-brother.[4] Unfortunately for some, home is not always a safe haven, but is the first place they experience the bitter taste of rejection, and they either develop the ability to prevail over it, or become consumed by its presence.

* * *

WORK

On any given week, the news outlets report on another tragic workplace shooting. The only change in the television coverage is that the people are different, but the scenarios are the same. A disgruntled former employee, upset with his poor performance review or frustrated with being passed over for promotion, takes out his aggravation on the employer or coworkers who he felt rejected him. Or the woman who can't seem to penetrate the corporate glass ceiling because of the rejection from her male peers, who deem her as inferior, relegating her instead to a mere object of their lustful admiration. Work, the very place you labor and sweat in an effort to receive compensation worthy of the services rendered, in turn can be a place of scorn, disdain, and dreadful rejection.

* * *

PLACE OF WORSHIP

Recently, the news reported the story of a deacon who was facing criminal charges for pulling a knife on another deacon at church while they were having a heated board meeting. Thankfully, no one was injured, but it appears that feelings of rejection surfaced when one deacon did something the other deacon did not like, resulting

---

3   1 Sam. 17:28

4   2 Sam. 13

in one man's need to use violence. Some people are shocked that you will find hypocrisy, cliques, gossip, and self-righteous egotistical people all in the church! More and more often, places of worship are becoming sources of contention and rejection. Whether it is people looking down on you because you aren't dressed the way they'd like, or the ministry that you worked so hard to get off the ground that ultimately failed, or even the new convert who left the church because they were rejected by the saints instead of being embraced in their new walk with Christ. What happens when God's house is not a sanctuary? Being rejected in the church by the body of believers is unfortunately a common occurrence. The church is the one place where everyone should be in one accord—encouraging, loving, and lifting up each other in the Lord—not a source of agonizing rejection.

* * *

IN THE COMMUNITY

Like some children, one of my earliest experiences with rejection happened in the sixth grade at the beginning of the school year. The teacher instructed the class to assemble our desks in groups of five. After we followed her instructions and settled down in our group of five, the self-appointed group leader and class bully directed her attention towards me and said in a loud voice, "If any of our stuff, pencils, pens, erasers, and books are missing from our desks, we'll know that you are the one who stole it, so you better leave our things alone!"

As the rest of the students laughed in agreement, all I could do was bow my head in embarrassment, not because I was considered the class thief, who was going to pilfer through their school supplies, but because I discovered that their stereotype and rejection of me was based solely on the color of my skin.

The painful memory of their childish rejection still lingers in my mind, and there are many others who have faced isolation and indifference from the very society that boasts about its inclusion and impartiality. Many in our communities have experienced the treacherous trial of rejection, from the child bullied on the playground, to the customers encountering a salesman who frowns when they enter the store, acting as if they don't belong. These experiences of being a rejected social outcast deliver a personal blow that hurts and stings, regardless of the package in which it is wrapped.

* * *

CAN YOU HANDLE IT?

It is a common belief that people have an innate desire to be accepted and wanted. Research indicates that children thrive best when they are nurtured, loved, and valued. It is in this environment where they develop a sense of confidence, and as they grow and transition into adults, they embrace a life of security and a sense of belonging.

In contrast, rejection breeds sentiments of incompetency, as though you have fallen short and missed the mark of your targeted goal. No one likes being the object of rejection, not being able to achieve what you desired, and instead being seen as inept and inadequate. Believe it or not, rejection can be found everywhere you look. It is an inescapable part of life that everyone must face at one time or the other. From the minuscule, teenage crush that broke your heart, to the dream job you didn't get, to the emotionally excruciating denials of a parent who abandons their child, to the husband who leaves his wife for a younger woman, rejection abounds! Rejection remains an equal opportunity event, which can destroy even the strongest of minds. Regardless of how we look at it, *rejection* travels along life's journey with us, clinging tightly.

Experiencing rejection can be considered psychologically and physiologically painful. Researchers have found that physical pain and intense emotional pain activate the same pain-processing pathways in the brain, and that pain and social rejection may have overlapping sensory mechanisms in the brain. Through the use of magnetic resonance imaging (MRI), researchers found that the area of the brain associated with pain also lit up when participants recalled a rejection. These findings are consistent with the idea that the experience of social rejection may represent a distinct emotional experience that is uniquely associated with physical pain.[5]

As challenging as it seems, every rejection has a role in shaping your life, and how the experience is dealt with refines and unquestionably defines your character. Instead of accepting the rejection and examining it for what it is, many people retreat from it, missing the object lesson being taught and the opportunity stemming from it, which may very well lie below the surface. Instead of wielding the power within, the rejected relinquish their control, enabling the circumstances of their situation to have dominion. Ultimately, the power to change the perception of rejection and the role that it plays in life lies within. This unwavering stance can be a tremendous factor in understanding exactly what life may bring your way.

There are many notable people who have faced an abundance of rejection in their life but, due to their disposition and perception, did not let it deter them from the task at hand. For example, Thomas Edison, the early inventor, faced years of rejection and failure as he worked on inventing the electric light bulb. A popular story purports that Thomas Edison was interviewed by a young reporter, who boldly asked Mr. Edison if he felt like a failure, and if he thought he should just give up. Perplexed, Edison replied, "Young man, why would I feel like a failure? And why would I ever give up? I now know definitively over 9,000 ways that an electric light bulb will not work.

---

5   Kross, Ethan, Marc G. Bergman, Walter Mischel, Edward E. Smith, and Tor D. Wagner. "Social rejection shares somatosensory representations with physical pain." *Proceedings of the National Academy of Sciences of the United States of America* 108, no. 15 (April 12, 2011): 6270-275. doi:10.1073/pnas.1102693108.

Success is almost in my grasp."[6]

Shortly after this statement and after 10,000 attempts, Edison invented the light bulb. What an amazing lesson about rejection. In the face of a multitude of miscalculations and misinterpretations, he forged ahead, not deterred by his failures but encouraged about the prospects that lay ahead of him. While Thomas Edison could be considered the poster child for rejection, in spite of all his failures he did not give up. After his tenth try, he did not sulk and walk away, not even after his thousandth attempt. He continued on, knowing that despite his failed attempts he was learning something along the way that would make his ultimate product better than it ever could be.

Another example of inexhaustible perseverance in the face of rejection is the story of George Washington Carver, the famous African American inventor. Although his childhood was marked with traumatic events, he did not let his difficult beginnings quell his curiosity for learning. Despite the racial adversity he faced, his fervent desire for continuing education propelled him to seek out institutions of higher learning. In this quest, rejection would overshadow his desire, as the color of his skin pre-empted his acceptance into the school of his choice during the time of segregation. Nevertheless, he was not deterred, and in spite of rejection he continued his pursuit. Thankfully, through his dogged determination and sheer will, he eventually prevailed! A school was willing to take a chance on him, and he was elated! George Washington Carver proudly enrolled in Simpson College in Iowa as the first black student. Thanks to his faith in God, his will to be a champion over adversity, and his creativity and stick-to-itiveness, he was able to create several inventions that changed the way the world used an assortment of food items

The Beatles, are another prime and noteworthy example of the phenomenon of rejection. They remained resolute in spite of the door being closed in their face. The renowned, multimillion-

---

6   Wilson, Larry. "What Why When." Daniel Revelation Bible Studies. https://www.danielrevelationbiblestudies.com/whowhat2009.htm (accessed September 18, 2016).

dollar-selling music band were initially turned down for a recording contract by a dismissive music executive, who said he didn't see any talent in them! Another example to behold is that of the 44th President of the United States, Barack Obama. Prior to ascending to the highest office in the land, in 2002 President Obama made an unsuccessful bid for the United States House of Representatives, where he was overwhelmingly defeated.

All of these people faced rejection. The most important lesson than can be learned from them is that they did not give up, and they did not let it cripple and stop them. Can you imagine if they had succumbed to the adversity they faced? Society would never have known such conscientious ditties as "Imagine," "Give Peace a Chance," and "Yesterday." We would still be using kerosene lamps, the first African American president would never have made it to the White House, and the joys of peanut butter and jelly sandwiches might never have been known.

Even when you believe you are abandoned and alone, God still watches over you. Through the many disheartening moments that we face, the Lord is in His garden of love, pruning, shaping, and preparing His children to grow in Him. We must recognize that God always has impeccable timing, and that the Lord is waiting for the precise moment His strategic will can be fulfilled in our lives. While this process may be uncomfortable, the Holy Spirit pleads with you to not throw in the towel, and prods you along, begging you not to give up. You must recognize in every situation that the Lord is dependable and there is surety in trusting in Him. God has better things in store for you, but you must go through some thorny patches. This is necessary in order to behold the artistry of His handiwork and bask in the beauty of the predestined roses He has for you.

* * *

God's purpose for rejection

There is a story about a man who faced a great deal of adversity in his life. As a child, he was given up by his mother and secretly adopted by a wealthy family, who passed him off as their own. Later on, he found out the truth, that those whom he thought were his family members were not really biologically related. He discovered that his real family was very poor and considered lower class. In the midst of dealing with his identity crisis, he witnessed an incident that sent him into a fit of rage. One of his poor relatives was being physically attacked by one of the rich cronies he grew up with. He intervened to defend his family member and ended up beating and killing his rich acquaintance. Word of his transgression spread like wildfire, and people turned their backs on him; even the very one he was trying to defend disrespected and rejected him. When the patriarch of his rich adopted family found out what he did, a contract hit was put out on his life to avenge the slaying he committed.

Fearing for his life, he left the country, created a new identity, got married, had a family, and started a new life. In spite of living a good life safely away from the threat of his past, he spent much time in reflection, yearning to find out where he truly belonged. This unquenchable desire propelled him to cast his newfound life aside, and motivated him to return home to find his biological family. By the time of his return, the family size had increased significantly, and he noted that they were still poverty stricken, living in deplorable conditions as slaves. As he reconnected with his siblings and other family members, he felt compelled to do something to remedy their situation. He quickly took the lead and mapped out a strategy, much to the dislike of his newfound siblings, who thought they were better qualified to lead. Under his leadership the family was able to make progress, but not without family members murmuring and complaining and questioning his authority.

In spite of their stubbornness, he remained patient with them and went on to achieve great things to benefit his family and improve their living conditions. However, no matter what good he did, it never satisfied them, and they continued to lash out and complain against him until he could take no more. Out of frustration, he came to a breaking point and angrily lashed out, defying a directive that he had been given. Despite many years of faithful service, he was penalized for his actions and told that he would have to resign and forfeit all the benefits that he had planned to reap.

What an incredible story of riches to rags, from reclaiming his heritage to losing his inheritance. This poor man, from birth to adulthood, experienced one trial after another and just could not seem to catch a break. Does this story sound like a plotline in a fictional movie? Does it seem too farfetched? If so, read the story again, because it is a modern-day depiction of the biblical story of Moses.

* * *

Moses, the classic rejection case

Moses was given the awesome task of leading the children of Israel out of Egypt. God prophesied that Moses would accomplish something great, but getting to that point would definitely not be easy. Who knew that the hardship he experienced growing up would help to prepare him as he returned home, pleading with Egyptian leadership to let God's people go?

The unique aspect of this story is that the Lord told Moses that this request would be rejected by the almighty Pharaoh. The Lord said to Moses, "When you return to Egypt, see that you perform before Pharaoh all the wonders I have given you the power to do. *But I will harden his heart so that he will not let the people go.*"[7]

Basically, the Lord said, "Moses go to Egypt, ask for my people to be released, but by the way, I'm going to allow Pharaoh's heart to be hardened, and he will say no and reject you!" The question to ask

---

7   Exod. 4:21 NIV

is, why would the Lord tell Moses to do something, knowing that the king's heart would be hardened? What was the purpose in this exercise?

The Lord essentially gave Moses advance notice about what he would be up against when he approached Pharaoh. God knew that as Moses migrated with the children of Israel, they would be uncooperative and obstinate. The reason that Moses experienced so much hardship in his earlier years was so that the Lord could prepare him to deal with the bouts of rejection he would experience at the hands of the children of Israel.

God often protects us through rejection when we are not prepared for what He has predestined. There is a quote that says, "Fail to prepare, prepare to fail," and it is the character of a loving Savior to forewarn His people about what they will face. God tells the Christian believer that they will face rejection, obstacles, trials, and tribulations, and that "men shall revile you, and persecute you, and shall say all manner of evil against you falsely, for my sake."[8] Just by the nature of being a follower of Christ, you will experience some of what the Lord went through.

God does not leave His children hanging, though. He is not into creating shock value and surprises, because the Lord will never put more on us than we can bear.[9] These teaching moments are used by God to prepare, fine tune, and equip His children as they maneuver throughout the Christian journey, toward the Kingdom of Heaven. With every challenging moment, our faith should steadily increase with the realization that our help and ability to overcome rests at the feet of Jesus.

So, Moses knew what he was up against, but even knowing this information, he most likely did not feel any more comfortable or confident about the situation. Very rarely is rejection accepted and embraced, even when there is a known possibility that it could

8   Matt. 5:11 King James Version

9   1 Cor. 10:13 NIV

happen. Recognizing that God had the situation under control allowed Moses to forge ahead through the difficult attempts to free the children of Israel. With the Lord on his side, Moses knew that the rejection he faced before Pharaoh would serve a greater purpose, and ultimately it secured the protection of God's people.

* * *

YOU HAVE THE POWER!

We must recognize that the Lord allows certain challenges to come our way in order to strengthen us on our spiritual journey. These progressive muscle-building exercises provide lessons in humility, reflection, and, most of all, dependence on Christ. However, the enemy will attempt to use these circumstances to plant seeds of despondency, bitterness, anger, and doubt in our minds. Satan's objective is to have Christians feeling hopeless, abandoned, stuck in the quicksand of rejection while he spews lies that the Savior does not really care.

If we allow the Holy Spirit to unveil our eyes, we will see the heavenly host cheering us on, encouraging us not to succumb to the enemy's deceit. The Lord has equipped His children, with principles that can be applied to our lives, enabling adversity to serve its transformative purpose. While this may not be an easy task, it can help you to analyze your situation and enable you to unleash the power to overcome what God has given you. By doing so, depression and defeat lose their strongholds. No longer will fear linger in our lives when disappointment comes our way.

* * *

BIBLICAL PRINCIPLES FOR DEALING WITH ADVERSITY

It is good practice to analyze and reflect upon your rejection experience and ask questions such as, why did this happen? Did I move ahead of God's calling? Is this not the direction the Lord wants me to be in? Am I not prepared? Was the rejection a result of my disobedience? Did this situation happen for my own protection? Did I go through this so that my testimony can glorify God and help someone else? Was I rejected to increase my faith and draw me closer to God? What am I to learn from this experience?

Having the understanding that rejection can happen for several reasons is a great place to start. Like a good parent, the Lord recognizes that, sometimes, if He allowed you to have what you wanted, you could experience harm. This could result in you being led down the wrong path, or miss out on an even better opportunity that He wants to afford you. God permits *rejection* for your *protection!*

Rejection may help you pause, reflect, and seek out a better vision. Going through hardships can provide the opportunity for you to slow down and reexamine life's journey. You will often hear that when one door closes, another one opens. The closed door of a rejection can allow for a better door of possibilities to open. With an open mindset, the Lord can help you develop a new game plan. What was once a negative experience can now be viewed through the lens of inspired perspective. With this renewed vision, God can enlighten and show you things you've never dreamed of before. Believe it or not, rejection can help you *refocus.*

We often find ourselves in predicaments because we did things that we weren't supposed to do and ended up making a mess out of everything. Due to our recklessness, family and friends disassociate themselves with our situation, leaving us despondent. Instead of placing the blame for our downfall on external entities, looking introspectively we discover that sometimes the issues we encountered were nobody's fault but our own. If you allow it, this rejection experience can lead to acknowledging our missteps, and direct us to make amends. This course of action leads us on the path of forgiveness towards God, who has the power to change every situation. Rejection can prompt you to *repent.*

Sharing your rejection story and the road you took to overcome can help to save someone's life. Your experience can steer them away from a life of disappointment to one of peace and purpose in Christ. Testimonies require a test! Recalling how the Lord intervened in our lives is fuel that can help propel others through their test. We must always remember, if He did it before, He can do it again. As you *recall*[10] and testify of His goodness, you serve as a source of inspiration for those who are coming up the rough side of the mountain.

Many times, we just don't understand why we are going through the things that we are experiencing; it just doesn't make any sense, and the burden appears too heavy to bear. In times like these, we must cling to the blessed hope of a brighter day in Jesus Christ. While in this earthly realm we may never know the reasons for some of our trials, in the land bright and fair all of our toils will be worthwhile. In acknowledging that God has a purpose for our storm, we acquiesce to His sovereignty, and with faith-filled obedience we worship in spite of how bleak the situation may appear. *Rejoice* in advance, for the wall of rejection will be conquered, and your breakthrough is within grasp. In the midst of your trial give thanks, worship, and rejoice in the Lord, for He doeth all things well.[11] Worshipping Christ should be at the core of everything that we go through, and every situation should draw us closer to our loving Savior.

Simply taking a step back from your situation, examining hardships for what they are, and recognizing the purpose they play in your life unveil the remarkable power of God to move in even the direst of circumstances. By applying these principles, you will be given the power to overcome every obstacle and rejection you face in your life.

---

10   Lam. 3:21 KJV
11   Mark 7:37 KJV

Testimony One:
The Rejected Driver

For many young people, a true indication of maturity, liberation, and independence is when they have passed their driving test and received their driver's license. I was one of the many teens who just couldn't wait to get on the wide-open road and go wherever I wanted to travel. When the time came, I paid the money I had saved up to attend a local driving school and began a twelve-week driver's education course. Week after week, I sat in class listening to the instructor teach the various theoretical principles of driving. During class, my mind drifted as I looked out the window, watching the cars whizz by and wishing that I, too, could hit the highways and byways instead of sitting in what I thought was such a boring class.

The instructor must have sensed my boredom, and he took me aside one day after class with an offer I should have refused. He agreed to sign off on my remaining theory classes so that I could take the driving portion of the class. This would allow me to quickly move forward with taking my driving test in order to ultimately get my license. I was excited about this proposal and justified why I should do it—in my mind, I knew everything I needed to know about driving and didn't need anyone to tell me how to park and when to stop. Even though I knew it was wrong, I hastily agreed to his proposition and eagerly watched as he signed off on the classes that I had no intention of ever attending. Finally, it was time to take my driving test; I was ecstatic and confident, and couldn't wait to get on the road after passing the basic driving skills test.

Unfortunately, things did not turn out the way I envisioned, because at the conclusion of the test the examiner notified me that I failed my driving test. What? I couldn't understand why, and in my ignorance, I sat confused by this unexpected failure. I naively shrugged off my disappointment, psyched myself up, and counted down the customary waiting period before I could take the test again. Shockingly, I failed the test again! I could not believe that I had finally gotten the courage to try again, and instead of driving away with the prized driving license, I failed once again.

Each time I felt bold enough to take the test over, I proved to be unsuccessful, ultimately failing my driving test a total of four times! Devastated and hurt, I did not understand why I kept failing at something I should have breezed through. At the time, it just did not make any sense, until it finally hit me. I didn't get a chance to learn some of the theoretical driving principles that I needed because of the deception I participated in by never attending those classes. In the midst of my frustration over not passing my driving tests, I was finally able to see God's protective hand maneuvering my life. Quite possibly, those missed lessons would've have taught me invaluable concepts that I needed to be able to practically apply during my driving skills test.

As ashamed as I am now of my impatience and dishonesty, I realize that in my haste and ignorance the almighty Lord allowed me to fail my driving test each time in order to keep me off the road and protect me—or better yet, keep those I would've encountered on the highways safe from the harm and danger that my inexperienced driving might have caused. In this rejection, the Lord rebuked my actions and did not let them prosper. Yet still, in His infinite mercy, He protected me from hurting myself and others.

After my fourth failure over the course of a year, I took some time to reflect and remedy the situation by taking additional driving lessons to cover what I initially missed. I praised the Lord that, with this newfound knowledge and experience, on my fifth attempt at taking my driving test I was finally victorious! It's quite possible that I could've had my license on the first try if I had not been impatient and had gone through the driving class according to God's timing. Ultimately, in my haste I ended up sabotaging myself, delaying the desires of my heart from manifesting until God saw that I was fit and ready. I thanked the Lord for the lesson learned and, most of all, for His protection.

It is important to remember that stepping outside of His will just one iota could lead to devastating consequences. This invaluable life lesson taught me that our Heavenly Father is a God of decency and order, and we should never rush ahead of His will and timing in our lives.

PRINCIPLE 1
REJECTION-PROTECTION

SOMETIMES THE REJECTION WE EXPERIENCE EXISTS FOR US TO
SEE THE HANDIWORK OF GOD'S PROTECTION.

* * *

JOSEPH'S STORY

One of the most powerful stories of overcoming adversity in the Bible is that of Joseph, a young man who ended up protecting the lives of the very people who rejected him. As detailed in Genesis 37, the story is an epic and dramatic depiction of hardship if there ever was one. As an adolescent, Joseph's misfortunes begin when his older brothers, out of jealousy, throw him into a pit and afterwards sell him into slavery. Then he is falsely accused of molesting his boss's wife and thrown into jail. Despite the atrocities he faces, he comes out triumphant, paving the way for him to miraculously become the overseer of the land and save the lives of the family members who rejected him in his youth.

* * *

RELINQUISHING JOSEPH!

Joseph isn't a fool! From the time he is a little boy, he knows that there is something special about him, and that his life is destined for greatness. His problem is that he just can't keep this news to himself! As the son of Rachel, the favored wife, Joseph is the delight and apple of his father's eye:

"Jacob loved Joseph more than any of his other children because Joseph had been born to him in his old age. So one day Jacob had a special gift made for Joseph—a beautiful robe. But his brothers hated Joseph because their father loved him more than the rest of them. They couldn't say a kind word to him."[12]

Not only is Joseph the favorite child, but he is also beloved by God, who speaks to him in his dreams, and Joseph happily shares these revelations with anyone who will listen, much to their annoyance. Joseph's dreams usually depict family members having to bow down to him in servitude, which further infuriates his siblings. Joseph is also seen by his brothers as a goody-two-shoes and tattle-tale, who often reports to their father about their poor work ethic and misdeeds while out farming in the field. The perfect storm brews as his brothers writhe with anger and jealousy and set a plan into motion to bring about Joseph's downfall. One day, when his father sends him out into the field to check on his older brothers, they see him coming from a distance and plot his demise.

"'Here comes that dreamer!' they said to each other. 'Come now, let's kill him and throw him into one of these cisterns and say that a ferocious animal devoured him. Then we'll see what comes of his dreams.'"[13]

Thankfully, Reuben, one of the brothers, decides to intervene to save his life, and suggests that they throw him into a well instead of killing him. They don't know that Reuben plans to go back and rescue him. One can only imagine how confused Joseph must be as his brothers lunge for him and he struggles for dear life to be free of them. He eventually loses his grip as they overpower him, and he plummets to the bottom of the well.

---

12   Gen. 37:3-4 New Living Translation
13   Gen. 37:18-20

As he sits there, bewildered, he probably overhears them laughing with glee, happy to be rid of him, relieved of his grandiose visions. The questions that must have swirled around in Joseph's mind, as he sat in the dank, dark and musty well! *What's going on? What are they doing? Why are they doing this to me? How could they do this to me? What did I ever do to them? What's going to happen to me?* As Joseph sits and contemplates his fate, his brothers see a caravan of Ishmaelite spice traders and decide to sell Joseph to them as a slave rather than let him die. It's bad enough for siblings to not get along and be jealous, but to go as far as getting rid of you and selling you out—that's pretty devastating!

Joseph appears to have every right to be angry and distraught over the course of events. Joseph could throw himself a pity party over being victimized. Instead of being bitter and resentful and wallowing in the bitter pill life gives him, Joseph valiantly chooses to maintain a life of devoted service and faithfulness to his Savior. His most prized possession in that instant is no longer his coat of many colors, but the manner in which he responds to the tragic events of his life.

Just as his brothers think that they have relinquished their problem, Joseph finds himself surrendering as well. He realizes that he has no alternative but to continue to submit his will to that of his Heavenly Father. In the race of his life, Joseph strategically hands over the baton, purposefully placing it in the Master's hand to run the rest of the way for him. Joseph figuratively and spiritually changes hands, yielding his will and desire to that of the Lord, and trading his inner turmoil and pain for God-given peace of mind. At the precise moment Joseph allows the Lord to direct the course of his life, he receives victory over rejection, his captors, and his circumstances.

Surrendering to your experience with rejection, just as Joseph does, can help to ensure that you are not destroyed by the situation, but that you grow, enabling God to manifest His perfect will in your life. While there are many object lessons that can be gleaned from

Joseph's rejection, three of the most important principles revolve around his integrity, his ability to let go and let God, and finally, his desire to let love conquer all.

* * *

SOMETHING ABOUT . . . JOSEPH!

Joseph's journey takes him through a terrain of mountains and valleys, highs and lows, and through it all he holds his head high, and even as a servant, he never wavers in living an honorable life. The Bible does not describe whether Joseph questions the Lord, has an attitude, or even murmurs about the situations he faced. However, based on his recorded actions, it can be safely assumed that Joseph remains cool, calm, and collected, and through it all, his uncompromising character never wavers.

On his journey, Joseph changes from the cruel hands of his brothers, to those of Ishmaelite traders, to being sold into Egyptian slavery. As a slave in Egypt, Joseph becomes a servant of Potiphar, one of Pharaoh's officials and captain of the guard.

The Lord is with Joseph so that he prospers. "When his master saw that the Lord was with him and that the Lord gave him success in everything he did, Joseph found favor in his eyes and became his attendant. Potiphar put him in charge of his household and he entrusted to his care everything he owned. From the time he put him in charge of his household and of all that he owned, the Lord blessed the household of the Egyptian because of Joseph. The blessing of the Lord was on everything Potiphar had, both in the house and in the field. So Potiphar left everything he had in Joseph's care."[14]

What an interesting turn of events! One moment Joseph is sitting at the bottom of a cistern, sold into slavery, and in the next he is given favor and placed in charge of the very home he is held captive in! Even as a slave, he exhibits such authenticity and commitment

---

14   Gen. 39:3-6 NIV

that his master takes notice and grants him an elevated position in his household.

While it seems like Joseph is spared the fate his brothers originally intended for him, Joseph's encounter with rejection does not end in Potiphar's house. Not only does the master notice Joseph's goodness, so does the master's wife!

"Potiphar's wife soon noticed him. She asked him to make love to her, but he refused and said, 'My master isn't worried about anything in his house, because he has placed me in charge of everything he owns. No one in my master's house is more important than I am. The only thing he hasn't given me is you, and that's because you are his wife. I won't sin against God by doing such a terrible thing as this.'"[15] She begs Joseph day after day, but he refuses to do what she wants or even to go near her.

Talk about being honorable! Regardless of his physical location, whether it be at the bottom of a pit, beholden to his master as a slave, or being enticed to commit adultery, Joseph remains steadfast. In spite of his unwavering principles, he is met with even more rejection, as his master's jilted wife falsely accuses him of molesting her, resulting in Joseph being condemned and sent to prison.

* * *

JOSEPH'S UNREQUITED LOVE

Rejected and destitute, imprisoned for a crime that he did not even commit, Joseph's story takes on another twist as he interacts with two remarkable prisoners. Both the king's personal servant and his chief cook make the king angry, so he throws them into the same prison with Joseph.[16]

The king's servants have their own date with rejection, which proves to be an appointment with Joseph's destiny. While in prison,

---

15   Gen. 39:7-10 Contemporary English Version
16   Gen. 40:1-3 CV

the men are haunted by dreams that they cannot understand. This affords Joseph the opportunity to use his God-given interpretation skills to their advantage. Amazingly, at what could be perceived as another low point in his life, God uses Joseph as a vessel to help his fellow inmates. Joseph's display of talent is not without benefit to himself. After positively interpreting the Cupbearer's dream, Joseph appeals to his sense of humanity and says, "[W]hen these good things happen, please don't forget to tell the king about me, so I can get out of this place." Everything happens just as Joseph says it will, but the king's personal servant completely forgets about Joseph.[17]

Just when you think Joseph's story will take a turn for the better, things only get worse. The very person that Joseph helps obtain his freedom forgets about him, not even giving him a second thought. So, Joseph continues to swallow the bitter pill of life. Just how much more rejection can he take?

Somehow, something deters Joseph from being enveloped and drowned in a pool of disgust; the indomitable love Joseph finds in his Heavenly Father replaces the love denied him by humankind. Joseph permits the colossal spirit of God's love to steep and marinate in his heart, mind, and soul, enabling its altruistic power to safeguard him from the fiery darts of rejection that are unceasingly hurled at him. When the foundation of his life shakes, and he bemoans his state of being, the salve of love rescues and lifts Joseph far above his situation. The hymn "Love Lifted Me"[18] captures Joseph's journey and punctuates the powerful supremacy of God's love:

> *I was sinking deep in sin, far from the peaceful shore,*
> *Very deeply stained within, sinking to rise no more,*
> *But the Master of the sea heard my despairing cry,*
> *From the waters lifted me, now safe am I.*

---

17 Gen. 40:14 & 23 CV

18 Rowe, James. "Love Lifted Me," in *Worship & Song* edited by Lester Ruth. Nashville: Abingdon Press, 2011, no.3101.

Love lifted me! Love lifted me!
When nothing else could help
Love lifted me!
Souls in danger look above, Jesus completely saves,
He will lift you by His love, out of the angry waves.
He's the Master of the sea, billows His will obey,
He your Savior wants to be, be saved today
All my heart to Him I give, ever to Him I'll cling
In His blessèd presence live, ever His praises sing,
Love so mighty and so true, merits my soul's best songs,
Faithful, loving service too, to Him belongs.
Love lifted me! Love lifted me!
When nothing else could help
Love lifted me!

Joseph gets it right! He recognizes that only God's love can lift him from the chain of events that ensnarls his life. The love of God sustains him as he travails throughout the years, nourishing and keeping him as the enemy of life seeks to siphon him away. By feasting on the never-ending supply of love from God, Joseph embodies the principle that, no matter how much difficulty you face, you must hold up a loving standard through it all.

* * *

LOVE'S CROSSROAD

Finally, after what seems to be an eternity, Joseph triumphantly gets his breakthrough. Two years after he reveals his cellmate's dream and the cupbearer is restored to the king's side, Joseph's interpretative skills are once again called to the helm. This time it is the king who has a disturbing and perplexing dream, which places a melancholic mood over the kingdom.

"In the morning his mind was troubled, so he sent for all the magicians and wise men of Egypt. Pharaoh told them his dreams, but none could interpret them for him."[19] During this time, the cupbearer reminds the king about the time he was punished and thrown into prison. The cupbearer tells the king that while he was in prison, he too had a dream that he could not understand. The king's interest is piqued, and he listens as the cupbearer reveals how he told one of his fellow cellmates, a young and humble lad, about the bewildering dream. The prisoner was able to successfully interpret his dream and predict the cupbearer's very presence before the king. Joseph is immediately called out of the dungeon, brought before the king, and asked to interpret the king's dream. The Lord shows him favor, and Joseph accurately and prophetically interprets the king's dream.

"Seven years of great abundance are coming throughout the land of Egypt, but seven years of famine will follow them and all the abundance of Egypt will be forgotten and the famine will ravage the land. Let Pharaoh appoint a wise man and put him in charge of the land and take a fifth of the harvest during the years of abundance and place it in reserve. This food should be used during the seven years of famine so the country will not be destroyed during the famine."[20]

The king's dream forewarns that Egypt will experience a famine and possibly face significant ruin if they are not proactive in saving their land. The revelation of the dream illuminates the king's mind so that he heeds every word of Joseph's interpretation, immediately mobilizing the kingdom to act. In spite of all the rejection he has experienced, Joseph is now catapulted to the top of the king's command. His love for God, his veracity, and his solid business acumen all play a part in solidifying Joseph's future.

"Since God has made all this known to you, there is no one so discerning and wise as you. You shall be in charge of my palace, and all my people are to submit to your orders. Only with respect to the

---

19   Gen. 41:8 NIV

20   Gen. 41:29-36 NIV

throne will I be greater than you."[21]

Joseph is revered by the king because of his wisdom, and the king eventually appoints him as governor over the land. When his brothers discard him like trash at the bottom of a pit, God dusts him off and places him on higher ground. While his brothers see him as nothing but a troublemaker, the king sees a man filled with wisdom and virtue. Where his brothers are envious and jealous, the Lord God sees Joseph as a worthy instrument to be used for His glory. As Joseph goes from trial to tribulation, from slavery to the dungeon, the foundation of his character remains unshaken, and his unequivocal valor shines through brilliantly in every situation he faces.

The Bible states that the Lord is with Joseph, showing him mercy and favor.[22] No matter where he goes, Joseph's formidable character follows, and because of this, many prestigious honors are bestowed upon him, and Joseph always ends up as the head instead of the tail.[23] Joseph's testimony is perfect evidence that tests, trials, and tribulations can refine a person's character. By taking a page out of the exemplary story of Joseph, we too can live a life of humility and say, with blessed assurance, "May integrity and uprightness protect me, because my hope, Lord, is in you."[24]

Just like his brothers made a choice to get rid of their brother, Joseph has to decide to not allow the rejection he experiences to consume him. The issues of his past have no hold on him and cannot thwart the plans of the Master, as God protects him along the journey. We must remember that even in the direst of circumstances, God can turn your situation around to be used as a lesson of His love, grace, and mercy.

* * *

21   Gen. 41:39-40 NIV
22   Gen. 39:21
23   Deut. 28:13
24   Ps. 25:20-22

HIS REJECTION, THEIR PROTECTION!

While Joseph meets with many ill-fated circumstances, his brothers' outcome revolves around remorse and sorrow. The story continues that when the brothers see how utterly devastated their father is to learn that Joseph is gone, they amend their wicked ways. During the years Joseph is separated from his brothers, these sons of Jacob change in character. Envious, turbulent, deceptive, cruel, and revengeful they were; but now, when tested by adversity, they are shown to be unselfish, true to one another, devoted to their father, and, themselves middle-aged men, subject to his authority.[25]

Joseph's brothers have the chance to reflect on the harm they caused their brother, and the pain they inflicted on their father. Through divine intervention, their rejection of Joseph is the catalyst that softens their hearts, allowing them to experience genuine remorse, which changes their outlook on life.

Unbeknownst to Joseph, his interpretation of Pharaoh's dream will eventually bring him face to face with the siblings who once rejected him. As a young boy, he envisions that one day his siblings will bow down to him with regard and admiration. Joseph doesn't know that all of his past experiences will culminate in the literal manifestation of his dreams. Thanks to Joseph's foresight and planning, Pharaoh's kingdom isn't feeling the effects of the famine that devastates the remainder of the region. Joseph's family back in Canaan cannot say the same, and out of desperation, Jacob commands his sons to travel to Egypt and purchase food to sustain their families.

God perfectly times Joseph's climactic journey to coincide with his family's moment of greatest need. As the story unfolds, the siblings come face to face with Joseph and do not even recognize the brother they rejected, who stands so powerfully before them. Joseph immediately recognizes his brothers; their faces are seared

---

25 White, Ellen G., *Patriarchs and Prophets*. CreateSpace Independent Publishing Platform, 2010.

into his mind from the last time he saw them, while he begged and pleaded for mercy. Now, here they stand in his presence, begging for sustenance as he once begged for his life.

Joseph isn't going to be duped by his brothers again; he wants to see if they are the same conniving men who rejected him as a child. Due to God's perfect timing, Joseph is able to use several creative means to uncover their true character. When he ascertains that, indeed, they have changed, only then does he reveal himself to them.

"'Come close to me.' When they had done so, he said, 'I am your brother Joseph, the one you sold into Egypt! And now, do not be distressed and do not be angry with yourselves for selling me here, because it was to save lives that God sent me ahead of you [. . .] to preserve for you a remnant on earth and to save your lives by a great deliverance. So then, it was not you who sent me here, but God!'"[26]

You can imagine the confusion the brothers must feel to see Joseph alive and well. The last time they saw him, they were selling him into slavery on a caravan into Egypt. Now, years later, divinely appointed, he stands clothed in kingly regalia, holding the keys to their future. What heavy burden and guilt must be lifting from their shoulders as they fully realize God's master plan.

What they mean for bad, only the good Lord above can turn around for good. Joseph's rejection ultimately protects and saves his family's life.

* * *

It's not all about you!

The lesson to learn from rejection may not always be for the person being rejected, but rather for the individual doing the rejecting. Such is the case with Joseph and his brothers. Joseph does nothing wrong, yet he suffers horribly under the hands of his brothers. Their tactless and appalling behavior many years ago sets

---

26 Gen. 45:4-7 NLT

in motion a plan that results in Joseph ultimately saving their lives. Not only does their rejection of Joseph eventually save their lives on a physiological level by providing them nourishment during the famine, but indirectly his rejection also saves their lives spiritually.

Through divine providence, this experience serves as a pivotal moment in their lives, and haughtiness, jealousy, and hatred is replaced with concern, protection, and love. Joseph's brothers learn a critical life lesson when they reject Joseph. Dealing with the repercussions of what they did helps to refine their characters and whittle away the rough edges, prompting them to look at life differently. While they may not have passed the test the first time around, their rejection serves a purpose in Joseph's life as well as their own.

Despite whatever you are going through, be still, and know that the almighty God, the overseer, is maneuvering your life with purpose, strategically positioning you where you need to be, to protect yourself or someone else in your life. At the same time, the Lord is working to change the lives and hearts of those who denigrate and reject you. You can believe this to be true: in everything we experience, God's ultimate goal is to save souls, and the Lord will even do so through rejection.

PRINCIPLE 1: REJECTION—PROTECTION

REJECTION MAY APPEAR TO BE REJECTION,
BUT IT COULD BE A MANIFESTATION OF GOD'S PROTECTION.

1. How can my experience with rejection be viewed as
    a method of protection?

_____

_____

_____

2. What door is God allowing to be closed in my life?

_____

_____

_____

3. Can my rejection experience help someone else?
    If so, how can it help others?

_____

_____

_____

4. Is the Lord protecting me from something that I
    cannot see at this time in my life?

_____

_____

_____

5. Did my experience with rejection give me a detour
    to a better outcome?

_____

_____

_____

TESTIMONY TWO:

THE JOB I'VE ALWAYS WANTED

My mother-in-law had a lengthy career in social work serving children who were abused and neglected. Just as I did, she experienced burn-out with the job, and decided to leave the agency where she worked. After a few years passed, she received a phone call from the very same agency she left, requesting that she come back on an emergency basis to fill a certain position until they could hire someone permanently. She weighed this decision heavily and prayed about it, finally consenting to return to the agency. However, the Lord told her that this would not be a long-term arrangement.

This new position gave her flexibility to creatively meet the needs of community members, which allowed her a genuine sense of fulfillment at the agency. To her surprise, she truly enjoyed the work and felt that this position was a better fit. Many of her co-workers applauded her efforts and remarked about what a great job she was doing, encouraging her to apply for the permanent, full-time position.

She took their advice, applied for the position, was interviewed, and waited patiently to hear whether she got the job. All around her, colleagues and supervisors assured her that she was a shoo-in, since she was already doing an exceptional job in the position. However, to the shock and dismay of everyone, she didn't get the job! She was devastated and embarrassed to have to face co-workers, who thought she was a guarantee, only to discover that they had gone with another applicant. She was perplexed; they had asked her to come back, and here she was, actually doing the job and receiving all of this positive feedback, and they chose to hire someone else. The rejection just logically didn't make any sense . . . at the time. Then she remembered what the Lord told her months before.

This experience led my mother-in-law to sit back and reflect on what her purpose was. Eventually, she remembered what the Lord instilled in her heart long ago. For many years, she had fostered the dream to start her very own early learning center. She recalled how, through the years, she would save money to purchase toys and items for her daycare. Bit by bit, she would take these items and place them in storage to be used at a later time. Then the frenetic pace of life caught up with her, and she put her dream on hold, only wishfully thinking about it from time to time.

Somehow, not getting this job made her reflect on the seed God planted in her soul—to nurture and provide care for God's most impressionable children. The door of this job opportunity closing provided the motivation she needed to move forward with her dream. Despite her disappointment, she embarked on the journey the Lord planned for her so long ago. She could finally fulfill her calling and passion in a place where she could be the most effective, nurturing the minds of God's little lambs.

She excitedly put the Lord's plan into motion; she found a temporary job while compiling an inventory of the things she had purchased for her daycare through the years. She soon realized that God had already provided the things she needed to make her dream a reality. All she needed was children to fill the place with laughter.

We believe that the Lord's sense of humor and perfect timing manifested clearly in this situation, because just a few months after she opened for business, we were reserving our very own slot in her daycare—we were expecting our first child, her first grandchild! Oh, what a blessing it has been for her to spend precious time with her grandchild. Who better to provide care for a child in the absence of their parents than the loving, tender arms of a grandmother? God knew before we were even married that our daughter would thrive under the care of her grandmother, who needed rejection to nudge and motivate her into what He had called her to do.

My husband and I often joke that if our daughter had not received her early learning under the dutiful care of her grandmother, the only words she would know would be *ga-ga-goo-goo*, instead of being the bright and articulate child that she is now. We attribute this to the detailed, painstaking love and nurturing that my mother-in-law gave our daughter through her formative years. We praise God for the rejection she experienced, and the way it propelled her to where she needed to be, helping God's little children find the way they should go.[27]

---

27   Prov. 22:6 English Standard Version

PRINCIPLE 2:
REFOCUS

WHEN EXPERIENCING REJECTION, USE IT AS AN OPPORTUNITY
TO REFLECT AND FOCUS ON YOUR PURPOSE IN LIFE.

The story of Jonah is a vivid depiction of how an encounter with rejection can provide a renewed outlook on life. He exemplifies what can happen when you detour from the path God originally intended. Just like Jonah's circumstances, there are times when the Lord clearly gives you a task to complete. Unfortunately, we allow fear, disbelief, and stubbornness to deter us from fulfilling our divine assignment. As a consequence of our disobedience, we may experience bumps along our journey that come disguised in the form of rejection. Thankfully, as in Jonah's case, the Lord in His love and mercy uses surprising and innovative tactics to get us back on the right track.

* * *

STUBBORN REFUSAL

Jonah was a false advertiser! By profession, Jonah was a prophet, yet he did not want to do his job and prophesy. In the four brief chapters that chronicle Jonah's story, we are taken on an adventure by a hardheaded man who displays blatant disregard for orders from his boss. From the beginning of the first chapter, we are plunged into the storyline; the Lord gives Jonah clear instructions to deliver a message of repentance to the people of Nineveh. Jonah immediately assesses the assignment and refuses, believing that the Lord is sending him on an impossible mission.

The people in Nineveh are deeply enmeshed in a wicked lifestyle. Their secular culture is the complete opposite of all that is considered Godly, pure, and true. So corrupt and outlandish are their ways that even the most loving and patient God grows repulsed by their outright reckless and sinful behavior. The Lord, in His mercy, wants to rescue and save the Ninevites from damnation, and seeks out Jonah as the perfect candidate to plead with them to repent and receive salvation.

However, the ability that God sees in Jonah, Jonah does not see in himself, and, in turn, Jonah sees nothing worth saving in the people of Nineveh. From his perspective, the outlook appears bleak; he thinks it will be impossible for the people of Nineveh to reject their wicked ways. Jonah does not believe proclaiming this message from God will make an ounce of difference in their lives.

In essence, Jonah does not believe that God knows what He is doing! Jonah does not believe in people, does not believe in himself, and he doesn't believe in the power of God to bring about change in the lives of the Ninevites. Sadly, Jonah cannot even see that his stubborn refusal is comparable to the diabolical and sinful ways of the people of Nineveh. What an astonishing parallel between Jonah and the Ninevites! They are more alike in their disobedience than Jonah ever imagines.

Just as with Jonah, the Lord gives each of us an assignment. We are told to deliver an urgent message to those within our sphere of influence, a message to save and uplift souls. Unfortunately, instead of marveling at the privilege granted to us, we hesitate and analyze the logistics of the job. Instead of moving with haste and trusting the one who assigned the task, we immediately see the impracticality of what we are called to do. We try to take charge, egotistically placing the responsibility for the mission upon our fickle, man-made assumptions instead of realizing that our role is but a small part in a much larger operation. For some reason, we have the gift of imagining everything that can go wrong, rather than seeing, through the Almighty, what can go right.

With this doubtful frame of mind, we make no movement toward obedience. We are slow to realize that our stubbornness does not open doors, our defiance does not release blessings, and our dismissive nature does not yield any fruit. No good thing can come from our acts of rebellion; they only breed isolation, troubles, and rejection. Mercifully, despite our noncompliance, the Lord sees fit to use stubborn, broken, and deficient people to effect positive change for His Kingdom. Obedience to the Lord's call serves a dual purpose—to solidify our growth in Him, while casting lifesaving nets to someone else in need. God sees beyond our low faith-esteem to the potential that lies within us. The fact that the Lord entrusts us with the delicate task of implanting soul-saving seeds is nothing short of miraculous. Through the power of the Holy Spirit, we must fight against the same sin-induced, stubborn skepticism that consumes Jonah, and move with faith-filled obedience to accomplish the divine calling for our lives.

* * *

TROUBLE AT SEA

As the story goes, Jonah refuses to go to Nineveh, and instead chooses a path contrary to his assignment. By going in the opposite direction of Nineveh, he subconsciously sends a message to the Heavenly Host that he is god of his own life, and knows better than the omnipotent God. Unfortunately, Jonah finds out the hard way that for every action, there is a reaction, and there will be consequences for his poor decision-making.

By boarding a ship to Tarshish instead of Nineveh, Jonah defiantly travels far away from where the Lord intends for him to go. The farther away the boat travels, the more encounters with rejection Jonah experiences. The Lord, in His mercy, wants to provide Jonah with an opportunity to reconsider and reroute, so God sends a great storm to get back Jonah on course.

Jonah's contrary actions don't just affect him, but also those on the ship with him. As the winds and rough seas whip upon the boat, the sailors on the ship begin to fear for their lives and do whatever they can to steady the ship. They call out to their gods, throw items overboard, and run about in a frenzy to lighten the ship of whatever materials they can spare. Incredibly, Jonah is completely unaware of the uproar above him, as he is lulled into a deep sleep in the hull of the ship. His shipmates' attempts to combat the storm remain in vain, until Jonah, the root cause of the turbulence, becomes aware of the role he has played in the drama.

It bewilders the mind to think that Jonah can sleep when, all around him, chaos permeates the air. His sound sleep symbolizes his comfort and complacency in his decision to go against God's wishes. His obliviousness to the fate of those on the ship is like his ignorance regarding the urgent spiritual needs of the Ninevites. How dare he sleep when lives hang so precariously in the balance!

Jonah needs something to jar him back to reality, and it is the Captain's booming voice, demanding answers, that wakes him from his slumber. Attempting to maintain control of the ship, the captain instructs Jonah to help steady the boat, but without a command from the heavenly Captain of the sea, none of the captain's efforts prevail.

Instead of being forthright and acknowledging that he is the cause of the turmoil, Jonah sheepishly hangs back amid the din, seeking to remain awake, yet asleep to the peril at the fore. The winds and the waves clamor ferociously against the ship, sending it careening out of control. Desperately fearing for their lives, the sailors strategize to find the reason behind the sea's wrath. They cast lots, which shed light on the responsible culprit and finally expose

Jonah's transgressions. His fellow shipmates bombard him with questions; they hang onto his every word because their lives depend on his confession.

As bold as he is when countering God's request, Jonah now has a totally different demeanor. Jonah comes clean, telling the men that it is he who angered the God of the land and the sea with his disobedience. As he concludes his explanation, Jonah comes up with what he determines is the only viable solution, and proposes that his death can save their lives. He pleads for them to throw him overboard to be free of the havoc that his actions have wreaked upon the ship. In spite of his keen suggestion, the sailors seek to exhaust all other reasonable efforts rather than accept loss of life.

Remarkably, these men have more compassion in their hearts than Jonah, and they prefer to save his life, despite the fact that he is the cause of their plight. If only Jonah exhibited to the people of Nineveh the same merciful and salvific traits demonstrated by these men, they would not all be in this predicament. As the seas relentlessly churn and the storm refuses to cease, the seasoned sailors try everything in their power to return to land. Their efforts to combat the sea are futile; the situation grows worse by the minute, and they know that something has to give. Either they all perish at sea or they try the only thing they have not tried. As their last resort and only hope, they raise their voices in prayers and worship to God, demonstrating more courage than Jonah. Jonah says not a word, resigned to his fate.

The Bible states that the men on the ship, not Jonah, cry out to the Savior and petition the throne room. As they contemplate their only recourse—to cast away the problem—they beg the Lord's forgiveness. Not knowing that Jonah is indeed guilty, they plead to not be held accountable for his innocent blood. These men demonstrate a higher level of spirituality than Jonah the prophet. The compassion they display for the one who has endangered their lives is unearned. While in no way equal, their willingness to save the unworthy Jonah, even to their detriment, emulates Christ's gift to an undeserving mankind.

With reluctant spirits, they throw Jonah overboard and into the sea. The benefits are felt instantly. The volcanic sea comes to a sudden standstill and assumes a stance of peace and serenity. As divine fate will have it, the same Jonah who rejected the request of the true and living God is now ejected from the ship, rejected by his fellow man.

It's easy to look at Jonah's story with a critical lens and see all of the things that he did wrong. He represents disobedience, stubbornness, ego, and unfaithfulness, all traits that are typically criticized and frowned upon. However, Jonah's story is not meant to be judged, but rather read in a way that allows for self-reflection and understanding. Each of us, in our own way, demonstrates Jonah-like qualities, where we reek of stubborn defiance. We often stand ignorant of the work God wants to do in our lives, and unashamedly shun His directives as irrational. How foolish we are not to realize that the work is for our good and the enlightenment of others. Every assignment is hand-crafted by the Savior, specifically tailored to our unique character to bring out our best and save us.

God is not like us, with selfish motives, seeking what we can fleece from each other. The Lord's selfless intentions drive His request for us to complete our individualized assignment. Every mission the Lord sends us is meticulously planned out, with the goal of refining our character, edifying others, and fulfilling His will. Nothing can stop the plans the Lord sets before us except the one who is given the task! We can be the greatest benefit and the worst obstacle to advancing the work of God. Like Jonah, we who are so fearfully and wonderfully made[28] abscond in the opposite direction, allowing fear to misguide and serve as a compass of distraction.

In each circumstance, there is no mistaking the clarion call of God's voice, but sometimes we choose an unnecessarily difficult path, believing it to be easy. The farther we go from Christ-intended

---

28 Ps. 139:14 NIV

directions, the more detrimental and life-altering are the consequences we face as a result. The reverberations of our defiance can be felt near and far. Many live the day-to-day drama and repercussions of decisions made outside the confines of the Lord's will. Faking ignorance and choosing to sleep through the aftermath of poor decision-making in no way absolves the responsibility placed upon our shoulders.

Many times, the trouble facing others is a direct result of our reluctance to intervene in their lives and serve as a lifeline from the Lord. Our waywardness doesn't just affect us but also the people closest to us, who in many cases feel the brunt of our disobedience as we remain oblivious. Lives are at stake, and yet we often remain asleep at the wheel, complacent in our decision-making, yet perplexed at the imbalance it causes.

Remarkably, it is often those who don't have a relationship with the Lord, like Jonah's shipmates, who will call out in desperation and petition the throne room for mercy. Their faith-filled demonstration puts to shame the actions of those who profess to know the Lord yet blatantly refuse to acknowledge their role in the devastating turn of events in front of them. Mercifully, the Lord will reroute us, sending encounters our way to jolt us back into reality. These moments of awakening often come disguised in unwelcome ways, in the form of rejection. However, just like Jonah, we must realize that when we reject Christ's commands, personal rejection will soon follow.

* * *

Time Out!

While the people on the ship are saved from a perilous plight, Jonah's saga with rejection lingers. Jonah thinks that the sea will be his grave, but even death rejects him, as God spares Jonah's life once more. In another tireless demonstration of His mercy, the Lord provides Jonah with an unlikely refuge from deep within the sea.

"Now the Lord provided a huge fish to swallow Jonah, and Jonah was in the belly of the fish three days and three nights."[29] From bad to worse. What an inconceivable predicament Jonah finds himself in, as he roils about in the putrid belly of the fish. This mammoth creature of the sea should symbolize an end to Jonah; instead, it nestles and protects its refugee from harm. Jonah experiences an intermission of sorts from the conflict swirling in his head. Even in the unlikeliest of places, within the belly of a fish, miles beneath the sea, he cannot block out the steadfast beckoning of the Lord. While Jonah's lodging is less than desirable, it does provide him with an amenity that he neglected before—a view of his relationship with the Lord. In this fishy setting, he finds himself having an audience with God.

Jonah is now in a place where he is free to rummage the recesses of his mind and reflect upon the state that he is in. This is evidenced by his monologue and contrite prayer to God. "When my life was ebbing away, I remembered you, Lord, and my prayer rose to you."[30] With no place to go or options at his disposal, the only access Jonah has to the outside world is a link to the Savior.

Only in the midst of rejection, isolation, and desperation is Jonah ready to avail himself of the one true source of life, the Lord God Almighty. In his quest for free will, Jonah saunters away from his divine calling, yet the Lord strategically places diversions along the way to put him back on track. The respite in the fish gains Jonah's attention; however, it is Jonah's choice to see this intermission for the life-saving maneuver that it is.

As outlandish as it may seem, Jonah's lodging within the fish is time well spent, for it enables him to acknowledge the error of his ways. He cries out, "I am cast out of thy sight; yet I will look again toward thy holy temple."[31] Jonah incorrectly assumes that the Lord has abandoned him, when in reality it is Jonah who rejected the Lord.

---

29   Jon. 1:17

30   Jon. 2:7

31   Jon. 2:4 KJV

Jonah recognizes that he took his eyes off the prize, neglecting his higher calling, and in the bowels of the fish, Jonah miraculously looks to the light of his salvation. Jonah's time-out serves its purpose, and allows the reflection necessary to steer him back to a spiritual life.

In parenting circles, time-outs as a tool of redirection are often useful in gaining the attention of errant children. A time-out is an interruption from harmful activity; the person is placed in supervised isolation to give them an opportunity to reflect upon their destructive behavior. Just as earthly parents are tasked with re-aligning their children, our Heavenly Father lovingly refocuses his sons and daughters who need direction. In order to do so, many times the Lord in His mercy will give His children a time-out experience, so that they might reflect upon the results of their decision-making.

The use of unconventional corrective measures is a strategy frequently deployed to move God's children back in line with their divine calling. However, like little children forced into time-out, we spend the bulk of the time sulking and pouting about the interruption in our game-plan. Initially, we sit in the proverbial time-out chair and ponder the past, assuming that we did nothing to warrant this recess. It takes us a while to recognize the formidable opportunities that a time-out presents.

It is only after stewing and squirming in our seats that we surrender to our placement. With no other place to go, a window of clarity manifests that allows deeper understanding of the present situation. The time-out, once viewed as reprimand, is now an opportunity to reflect, strategize, and reorganize. Before, thoughts were clouded with the perceived unfairness of life and the present situation, but now greater understanding and awareness take center stage. With the full realization that your detour is in the past, and no longer tempted to venture off the beaten path, you find true freedom now in grasp. A desire to please and submit to the one who humbled you permeates, and the rejection that once stung is soothed with the emergence of renewed focus.

* * *

THE MESSAGE, NOT THE MESSENGER!

What an astonishing miracle! Jonah, cast into the stormy sea and swallowed by a fish, spends three days and nights churning about in this mammoth beast, then has his life spared after being vomited onto dry land.

It's amazing what time spent in the belly of a fish can do to provide perspective and laser focus.

As he seeks to gain his footing, Jonah stumbles, shaking off the fish innards, and when, caught between awe and disgust, he rubs his eyes and clears his ears, the very first sound he hears happens to be the ringing voice of God, commanding once again, "Go to the great city of Nineveh and proclaim to it the message I give you."[32]

This time around, Jonah's response is significantly different. Jonah the unreliable messenger initially makes the message about him, and in return meets a fate filled with rejection, but he isn't supposed to worry about what type of reception he'll receive from the Ninevites, nor concern himself with the outcome of the message. The expectation is for him to do his part, leaving the rest in God's capable hands. The message is powerful on its own, and needs no messenger to dilute, retract, or renege on its delivery.

Now, with a heightened sense, Jonah hears the message loud and clear and, without hesitation, takes off, this time in the direction of Nineveh. Focused on the mission at hand, no longer is Jonah concerned about himself and his feelings on the assignment. The message takes precedence over everything else. With the newfound realization that the message is more important that the messenger, Jonah makes the choice to move out of the way and deliver the Word given to him.

Thankfully, the trauma he goes through allows him to regain focus. With a second chance and renewed energy, clarity and speed

---

32   Jon. 3:2 NIV

propel him toward the fulfillment of his divine calling in Nineveh. With the messenger in the background and the message front and center, Jonah, as a vessel of repentance, does an outstanding job sharing the Lord's information with haste, sincerity, and obedience. Jonah's message is so rousing and touching that the people of Nineveh mobilize into action, proclaiming a fast of repentance, seeking mercy from God.

"When the Lord saw what they did and how they earnestly sought to turn from their evil ways, He relented and did not bring on them the destruction he had threatened."[33]

What is little truly becomes much when placed in the Master's hand, because Jonah's efforts reap a bountiful harvest in the people of Nineveh, who atone for their wicked ways. Based on Jonah's dire message of repentance, amplified with the power of the Holy Spirit, the Ninevites relinquish their sin for the gift of salvation. The time Jonah spends away, rejected and alone, provides motivation to fulfill the task at hand—Christ's divine plan.

Like Jonah, we have all been given an urgent message from the Lord to share. The message is transformative and lifesaving, not only for the messenger, but also for those who will hear. Instead of marching onward in pursuit of ears to hear the message, precious time is wasted in resistance and futile contemplation. Souls depend upon your obedience to bring the message of salvation. Too much emphasis is placed on the messenger and the receptivity of the listeners, rather than the illuminating power of the message. To ensure that the message is delivered and barriers to its launch removed, the messenger must inevitably conquer rejection; rejection serves as a compass for the one who does not even realize they are lost, and is merely a temporary obstruction, ultimately providing the messenger a panoramic assessment of their situation. It is often through this very necessary and painstaking process that genuine self-analysis can occur, redefining the spiritual trajectory.

---

33   Jon. 3:10 NLT

Blessings reign upon those who travail stark experiences and, in obedience, regain their footing, to maneuver now with renewed perspective and zeal. Lives are saved because of Jonah's suffering. How many more lives can be saved by the door that closes or the distraction that momentarily sweeps you off course? Such experiences provide the opportunity to adjust the lens of your outlook, and provide the distinctive perspective needed to reignite your purpose.

The divine assignment Christ entrusts to you is the message you are to deliver, and an appointment with rejection is what you will encounter until you have refocused on the task at hand. The power behind the message can only be fulfilled once it is delivered in earnest. The source of the message is omniscient, containing the power to envelope and transcend the messenger; however, the messenger must choose to receive the message and to deliver it.

PRINCIPLE 2: REFOCUS—VISION

When experiencing rejection, embrace the opportunity to reflect and focus on your genuine purpose.

1. Am I walking in my Divine calling?

   _____

   _____

   _____

2. Do I feel as though I have "hit a brick wall" or am "stuck in a rut"?

   _____

   _____

   _____

3. Could I be experiencing rejection because I am running away from my divine assignment?

   _____

   _____

   _____

4. Has the rejection I've experienced brought about a renewed focus?

_____

_____

_____

5. What do I need to change in my life that will allow me to refocus?

_____

_____

_____

Testimony Three:

What God has for me, it is for me![34]

Dear 1234 Main Street Home Owner,

We first came in contact with this home prior to it being renovated. I would frequently drive by as I transported the foster children I worked with to the home of their foster parents, who lived down the street from 1234 Main Street. Week after week, I watched the progress diligently, as the home was purchased and then transformed before my eyes. I told my husband about this home and how it looked before. Now, mind you, I had only seen the outside and did not know anything about how the inside looked yet; still, this home piqued my interest.

Eventually we saw the home go on the market, and I told my husband about the open house that was scheduled to take place. We decided to attend and we were blown away by how beautiful the home was and the craftsmanship that was skillfully displayed in every room. We marveled at how the home met our needs, and discussed how we would arrange furniture. We believe that with the meticulous detail in which you refurbished the home, you had a special family in mind, and we know that we are that special family.

---

34 Miami Mass Choir. "It Is For Me." *It's Praying Time.* Savoy, 1997.

My husband and I will be married for three years in June, and this past October, we welcomed our first child, a beautiful daughter who is now six months old. From the time we got married, we dreamed about being first-time home buyers, and now that we have seen 1234 Main Street, we would love for it to be our first home together. We qualified for a home loan and would like to put in a bid to purchase this home. While we may not be able to pay the asking price, we are asking for you to take into consideration our situation, how much we love and appreciate the beauty of the home, and the tender care we would give this property. If you would be so kind and approve our loan, you would be playing a tremendous role in helping to make our dream come true of being first-time home buyers, and helping to leave a tremendous legacy for our family for years to come.

Thank you.

Respectfully Submitted,
Micah & Cheryl Chavers

* * *

This was the exact letter that we submitted to the property owner, along with our contract bid on the home; little did we know at the time that the rejection we were about to face was actually God's way of protecting us. We were so excited about this place and positive that it was right for us that I even did some detective work, and found the property owner's home number in the phone book. I called him to express our interest in the home, to hopefully sway his decision regarding our bid on the house. This was a taboo move on our part, because in the real estate industry you should never contact the property owner directly; you are supposed to go through the realtor. The gentleman took my phone call and I quickly introduced myself and raved about how beautiful the home was and what a perfect fit it would be for our family. He kindly listened and then suggested that I put in a bid for the home and contact his real estate agent right away.

We met with our broker and real estate agent and told them how much we loved the house, and that we wanted to put a bid on it. They responded to us in a respectful yet skeptical way, saying that the house cost more than what we qualified for in loans, and that most likely our bid would not be accepted. We told them that we knew that the house was outside the scope of our budget, and shared with them that we were Bible-believing Christians, who had faith in God, and that if the Lord wanted us to have this house, He would make a way, no matter what the house cost.

After our spiel, the realtor said that she would do as we requested, and recommended that, alongside the contract, we submit a letter of interest to be given to the seller's agent, explaining our situation. We prayed and prayed, waiting with anticipation for a miracle to occur. We knew in our hearts that our heavenly Father owned cattle on a thousand hills, and that the Lord would provide for us. We justified our actions by saying that the Lord wants us to boldly approach his throne, and that by stepping out on faith, surely the Lord would grant us the desires of our heart.

The next day we received a disappointing phone call from our realtor, stating that they had denied our bid, so emphatically that the seller's agent drew a large red line across our contract, turning down our application. We were heartbroken. Here we had stepped out on faith, and we didn't understand why the Lord didn't honor our request, knowing how much we wanted this home and how perfect it was for our family and how easily it could be used for ministry. Despite our disappointment, we trudged along with our housing search, and eventually found a lovely home that was in our budget and suited us perfectly.

As we settled into our new home and went about our daily lives, we would drive by 1234 Main Street and notice that the *For Sale* sign was still up in the front yard and the home remained vacant.

We were truly perplexed, and wondered why, since it appeared to be such a nice place. Several months later, I went to the home of the foster parent who lived down the street from 1234 Main Street. As I spoke with her, I noticed that she seemed anxious and troubled. She mentioned that she was getting ready for a local neighborhood watch meeting to discuss the recent wave of criminal activity taking place on their street.

She said that, in years past, the neighborhood had been well established and highly regarded, but recently the area had been experiencing break-ins, property damage, and stolen vehicles. What she said next got my full attention. She mentioned that down the street from her home, right in front of 1234 Main Street, prostitutes and drug dealers were hanging out on the corner, and that there had been several drug busts by police on that property that had been in the news. She said residents no longer felt safe, and that they were ramping up patrol in the neighborhood in order to fight back the wave of crime besieging their community.

I could not believe my ears. This house and neighborhood that we *thought* would be idyllic and the perfect setting for our family was actually quite the opposite! I rushed home and shared the news with my husband, and together, with this newfound understanding, we thanked God for the rejection we experienced. The Lord, in His omniscience, knew that area would not be safe for us to raise our family, and didn't want the house to bring any undue stress to us. In retrospect, we realized that we weren't turned down because we did not have enough faith, but because God wanted to protect us! As Christians, oftentimes we question the "walk by faith" concept and become frustrated with God when things do not go our way. The doors we wish would open are often closed, and eventually we realize the purpose behind the rejection. What resounds loudly through this situation is that God's purpose and protection in our life is for our good, and ultimately for His glory. Trust Him in all things!

PRINCIPLE 3:
REPENT—FORGIVENESS

THE PROPHET BALAAM AND HIS DONKEY

Many times, the rejection we face is the result of someone doing something to us. Whether it is a loved one hurting us or a closed door, the rejection we experience typically is out of our control. However, rejection is not always about external forces bringing calamity your way. What happens when you bring it upon yourself? More often than not, the rejection we go through is self-inflicted. This is the case with the Biblical prophet, Balaam, whose rejection by a donkey changed his life.

Numbers 22 tells the incredible story of the conflict between the Moabites and the children of Israel. Balak, king of the Moabites, is greatly concerned about the proximity of the mighty children of Israel to his people. He fears that one day the Israelites will overtake them and destroy his kingdom. This anxiety makes King Balak quite frustrated, to the point that he swiftly decides to do something about it. After much consideration, Balaam, a Gentile prophet, is called on the king's behalf to curse the children of Israel, with the hope that it will stifle their power and prevent them from prospering and overtaking the Moabites. In consideration of this request, Balaam proceeds to ask God's opinion on the matter, and from that moment on, he is taken on a challenging and self-reflective journey. Several interesting things happen to Balaam throughout his voyage that can teach us about rejection.

* * *

THE NEED TO FEED HIS GREED

When you think about what a prophet does, you think of someone who is wise, spiritual, and on a mission delivering messages from the Lord. Even though Balaam is considered a prophet, for some reason he lives a life contrary to these attributes. Balaam always looks to fill his coffers, with a "do for me and I'll tell you what I can do for you" mentality. Instead of standing out, being a bold and courageous servant of the Lord and letting God supply his needs, Balaam has a plan of his own.

Balaam has the gift of divination, also known as foretelling, and he is highly regarded throughout the land for his skills. King Balak sends prestigious and honorable men from his kingdom to persuade Balaam to curse the Israelites, with the promise of a substantial fee for rendering his service. Upon their arrival, they inform Balaam of the mission's directives. As he contemplates their offer, he remarks that he wants to confer with God first and then get back to them with an answer. Even though Balaam has questionable intentions, he still has the sense to consult God. "'Spend the night here,' Balaam said to them, 'and I will report back to you with the answer the Lord gives me.'"[35]

That night, the Lord comes to Balaam, and God instructs Balaam that it is not in His will for the children of Israel to be cursed, for they are a blessed and chosen people. From there, Balaam reports back to the king's entourage that he will not be able to go with them because the Lord will not give him permission. King Balak refuses to take no for an answer, and sends even more notable and prestigious men from his court to persuade Balaam to do his deeds.

---

35   Num. 22:8 NIV

This time around, Balaam's response to the king's men sounds promisingly resolute. "Even if Balak gave me his palace filled with silver and gold, I could not do anything great or small to go beyond the command of the Lord my God."[36] Balaam says all of the right things; however, his actions dictate his true intentions, as he instructs the king's men to rest for the night while he confers once again with God about what to do. Deep down, Balaam is really only interested in the reward from the king, and he is secretly hoping that the Lord will change His mind.

This is Balaam's most monumental mistake. His hidden intentions set him down the road to his first encounter with rejection. Balaam is just like a little child nagging his parents to get what he wants; he continues to ask God about what he should do, as if he didn't hear the Lord's response the first time. What more is there to ask? What can possibly have changed? Can God be bribed by the riches of this world as easily as Balaam is enticed by the king's offerings? No!

Balaam should know better—should know that God's standards never change, and that the Lord means what He says. "God is not human, that he should lie, not a human being, that he should change His mind."[37]

* * *

DONKEY BUSINESS

Despite God's initial veto, Balaam continues on his quest, hoping that the Lord will change His mind so that Balaam can partake in the rewards that Moab offers. "God came to Balaam in the night and said to him, 'If the men have come to summon you, arise and go with them. But you must do only what I tell you to do.'"[38] God's pronouncement pleases Balaam greatly. He saddles up his donkey

---

36   Num. 22:18
37   Num. 23:19
38   Num. 22:20 Common English Bible

and sets off on a road trip to see King Balak, envisioning the fortune that will be set before him. However, there is a slight twist in the story, because "God was very angry when he went and the angel of the Lord stood in the road to oppose him."[39]

Balaam is told to go, but he is instructed to go only if the men from Moab call upon him again. Balaam's greed overrules the instructions of the Lord, and fuels his haste to go on this journey. God's anger is kindled against Balaam because He knows that, at the core of Balaam's character, he is wishy-washy and easily swayed by King Balak. The Lord sees the root of Balaam's intentions, and that he is more interested in obtaining the reward of earthly goods than following the precise instructions the Lord gives to him.

As eager as Balaam is to get to his destination, God is equally adamant that he will not do the king's bidding. In His infinite mercy, God sends an angel to run interference and block Balaam's path. As Balaam and his donkey move forward, he is not able to see the angel of the Lord that is right before his eyes. However, "when the donkey saw the angel of the Lord standing in the road with a drawn sword in his hand, it turned off the road into a field. Balaam beat it to get it back on the road."[40]

Balaam's hastiness to promote his self-interests blocks his ability to see that his life is in jeopardy. He is so caught up in collecting the reward that he does not realize that the donkey's noncompliance is steering him away from impending doom. Balaam continues on his journey, ignorant to the angel of the Lord standing in the way with instructions to execute him. As the donkey saunters forward through the narrow pathway with walls on either side, he sees the angel of the Lord once again. Wanting to protect his master and save his life, the donkey maneuvers away, crushing Balaam's foot against the stone wall. The donkey's gesture is a helpful one that unfortunately has the opposite effect.

---

39   Num. 22:22 NIV
40   Num. 22:23

In outrage, Balaam lashes out and beats the donkey again for thwarting his progress and preventing him from moving on in his journey to self-fulfillment. Oblivious to the throbbing pain in his foot, Balaam is unable to equate his own stubbornness with the donkey's behavior. Here, Balaam is a self-professed prophet, and yet he cannot forecast the danger before him. It isn't that Balaam could not see the angel of the Lord standing before him; he chooses to turn a blind eye. The farther he goes on his journey, the more he tunes out the instructions of the Lord. He allows greed to dull his senses, producing visual and spiritual blindness.

While Balaam and his faithful donkey are on the same journey, heading in an identical direction, each has vastly contrasting missions. Stopped at a crossroads, both Balaam and the donkey experience rejection that stifles their ability to fulfill their tasks. However, the donkey's inflexibility is born out of concern, devotion, and protectiveness, whereas the root of Balaam's hardheartedness stems from immoral, sanctimonious, and self-motivated desires. The donkey's rejection of Balaam's commands is similar to Balaam's dismissal of God's holy instructions. Unfortunately, he is unable to see the connection. The farther he proceeds on his journey to self-indulgence, the more the donkey rejects him, slothfully moving down the road.

Once again, the donkey sees the angel of the Lord, and for a third time it stops dead in its tracks, immovable despite the wrath of his master, who rains blow upon blow on the innocent donkey. At this time, the Lord opens the donkey's mouth and it says, "What have I done to you to make you beat me these three times?"[41] As astonishing and miraculous as it is for an animal to talk, Balaam completely misses the phenomenon and, in a demeaning tone, actually responds to the talking donkey, full of pride and anger, blaming the donkey for making him look like a fool.

---

41   Num. 22:28 NIV

The furious Balaam spews out a venomous threat that he would kill the donkey if he only had a sword—the very same object the angel of the Lord now holds, and which the donkey is preventing his master from being slayed with. The story then reveals the significant history and special relationship between them, as the donkey says to Balaam, "Am I not your donkey, on which you have ridden all your life long to this day? Is it my habit to treat you this way?" And he said, "No."[42]

This dialogue between man and animal proves to be a turning point for Balaam. For years, this devoted and dependable donkey serves as a mode of transportation, journeying to and fro with Balaam as he prophesies throughout the land, steadfastly remaining by his master's side. While Balaam knows his donkey to be reliable, on this one occasion of obstinance, he discounts the donkey's years of faithful servitude and devotion, just to satisfy his selfish desires. At that moment, the Lord steps in and opens Balaam's eyes to the angel of the Lord. Balaam's sudden awareness of his ignorance brings him to his knees, and he listens as the Lord's messenger chastises him.

"Why have you beaten your donkey these three times? I have come here to oppose you because your path is a reckless one before me. The donkey saw me and turned away from me these three times. If it had not turned away I would certainly have killed you by now, but I would have spared it."[43]

In comparison to the story of Jesus, Balaam abuses and misuses the donkey, just as, years later, Jesus is maltreated and crucified, when all He wants to do is save mankind. What is given as a blessing and to serve as a salvific tool is seen instead as a threat and impediment. Likewise, Balaam's faithful donkey only wants to save the life of his errant master. Thankfully, in both accounts, the rejection faced does not thwart the Master's ultimate plan.

---

42   Num. 22:30 ESV
43   Num. 22:32-33 NIV

* * *

REPENT FOR THE EVENT

At this juncture, Balaam is able to reflect on the donkey's many attempts to intervene and save his life. By clearly seeing how greed, self-promotion, and disobedience might have gotten him killed, Balaam places things in perspective, finally remembering his original purpose for traveling to Moab. This understanding prompts him to utter three of the most powerful words that Balaam could say: "I have sinned."[44] This realization transforms Balaam, and for the first time, he acknowledges his wrongdoing. Balaam can no longer blame external forces for his tribulations; the rejection he experiences is a direct result of his actions, and not the donkey's stubbornness. "Your sins have been your downfall!"[45]

The miracle in this story is not that the donkey spoke, but that Balaam finally listened! After the Lord's repeated attempts to get his attention, Balaam sees the error of his ways and is able to grasp the powerful concept of rejection, repentance, and redemption. Mercifully, with a penitent heart, he changes the intentions of God from anger and death to acceptance and life. Balaam's mindset changes, and he wholeheartedly expresses this when he repents for his egotistical conduct. Not only does he repent and profess this conversion with his mouth, but his actions follow suit when Balaam says, "I did not realize you were standing in the road to oppose me. Now if you are displeased I will go back."[46]

Balaam's gesture speaks volumes and shows his willingness to make a complete turnaround. The reward from King Balak, which initially looms large in his future, now fades into the background and pales in comparison to the Lord's glory. Not only is Balaam cognizant of his mistake, he now earnestly attempts to remedy his actions by

---

44   Num. 22:34

45   Hosea 14:1

46   Num. 22:34

any means necessary. His swift internal transformation is reflected by his external expression of repentance and acknowledgement of the things that he has done. Balaam's newfound humility and meekness demonstrates this change, along with his sincere desire to make amends. Balaam now thrusts his life into the hands of the Lord, with a malleable willingness to be used according to God's wishes. "The angel of the Lord said to Balaam, 'Go with the men, but speak only what I tell you.' So Balaam went with Balak's officials."[47]

As the story unfolds, the Bible records that even though Balaam went to the city of Moab, he was obedient to the will of God, and much to the chagrin of the king, he refused to follow his orders. In this instance, Balaam's conviction holds strong, and despite the continued efforts of King Balak to buy him with promises of gifts and honor, Balaam allows himself to be used only as an instrument of the Lord, delivering blessings to the children of Israel instead of curses.

Balaam's journey can teach us powerful lessons about rejection and how it can be self-inflicted. Plain and simple, selfishness can cause rejection. Being selfish not only brings about personal ramifications, but directly and negatively impacts others in our lives as well. Placing our own agenda ahead of God's call only brings about trials and tribulations. Just like Balaam, many of God's children extol the Lord's virtues and profess Him with their mouth; however, sinful nature incessantly promotes tendencies that exploit the gifts of God for self-gain.

God's instructions for our lives are clear and concise, yet our stubbornness and selfish desires bring about ambiguity and confusion about what God expects from His children. We often attempt to pull God in to mediate the battle that rages within, with the hope that we can manipulate God to do our will. Just like Balaam's actions proved to be hypocritical and self-absorbed, many of God's people have sealed their fate by chasing desires contrary to the will of God, and not listening to God's instruction the first time. Similar

---

47   Num. 22:35

to the intimate relationship that begins with several red flags, yet recklessly continues down the slippery slope, all the while bartering and bargaining with God to change His mind and bless what the Lord already said would be cursed. How many divorces would have been prevented, or business partnerships quickly dissolved, if God's initial instruction had been heeded?

Instead, a mounting wall of rejection is faced with confusion. Our Heavenly Father can foretell the rejection and turbulence that will happen as a consequence of disobedience, and the Lord God is not pleased when His loving and preventative directions are not followed.

It is important to repent and ask for forgiveness when you recognize, like Balaam, that the rejection you experienced lies squarely on your shoulders. Balaam blames the donkey for rejecting his instruction, when all along, Balaam's own actions are the source of his troubles. The donkey is merely an instrument of God to get Balaam's attention. Similarly, many may feel that their family members, friends, employers, and others are to blame. Just like Balaam blamed the donkey, we blame others for the adverse experience. Upon closer examination, you may realize that you are the very cause for the rejection you now face. Taking responsibility for your actions is always a step in the right direction, and helps to clarify exactly where things went wrong.

It is also important to repent for the pain that your actions have caused others. Stubbornly attempting to handle things on your own makes things worse, and only strengthens rejection's grip. Not only did Balaam's disobedience affect him, but it also had an impact on those around him. Even though the donkey was innocent, the animal still suffered tremendously as he was beaten over the head and tormented. Likewise, Balaam's foot was crushed and bruised along the journey. Just like in the Garden of Eden and the fall of mankind, when sin occurs, everyone in the environment is affected.

After being rebuffed by his donkey and acknowledging his

selfish ways, Balaam sees his role in the rejection. The rejection Balaam experienced was a result of his disobedience, and he had to repent in order to make things right! In doing so, Balaam testifies to the prevailing power of God and how the Lord's way always leads to a better place. Honestly, admitting to God what you did, why you did it, and the pain it caused opens up a dialogue with your Maker so that He can help you deal with the repercussions of your rejection. Asking for forgiveness and repenting enables God's mercy to flow and shield the blow of consequences that may have to be endured. This act of repentance shows the Lord and others you have impacted that you are genuinely repentant for what was done, with no desire to do it again.

Repentance and prayerfully pleading with the Lord is the key to unlocking the chains of rejection that trap you and your loved ones. Acceptance of responsibility and repentance go hand in hand and produce genuine remorse. Most importantly, in God's eyes, repentance repels the stain of rejection and presents you pure and blameless before Him.

Stepping beyond your circumstance and reflecting on yourself can help you get to the true root of the problem. While this can be a challenging task, it is one of the most important steps in making amends. Being in denial about the cause of the rejection only serves to stifle progress. It also significantly hinders God's ability to manifest change in your situation. Once you allow God to deal with you, the Lord can then help you recover and set you on the road to making wiser and better decisions. While rejection can be considered a setback, repenting can help you move beyond your misdeeds and into a place where God can use you once again for His glory.

PRINCIPLE 3: REPENT—FORGIVENESS

REJECTION CAN OFTEN MANIFEST BECAUSE OF OUR OWN ACTIONS AS WELL AS NOT BEING OBEDIENT TO GOD'S WILL. WE SHOULD REFLECT AND EVALUATE OUR BEHAVIOR WHILE REPENTING FOR OUR DISOBEDIENCE.

1. What actions do I need to repent for?

_____

_____

_____

2. Did I blatantly go against God's will?

_____

_____

_____

3. Have I acknowledged my role in causing this rejection experience?

_____

_____

_____

4. Have I asked God for forgiveness for my actions?

_____

_____

_____

5. Have my actions impacted other people, and have I asked them to forgive me for the harm I may have caused them?

_____

_____

_____

6. Am I truly repentant for my actions and behavior, and am I willing to change and try and make this situation right?

_____

_____

_____

TESTIMONY FOUR
TRAGEDY TO TRIUMPH

A few years ago, I attended a conference where the keynote speaker was Dr. Terry Morris, a renowned NASA Rocket Scientist. He shared his testimony—how as a child he was physically abused, neglected, and abandoned by his family, eventually ending up in the foster care system. His ordeal began after his biological father deserted the family, and his mother singled Terry out from amongst his siblings and directed her anger and frustration towards him. From the time he was four years old until he was fourteen, he was mistreated by family members and was the target of their abuse. His mother would frequently dig her nails into his neck, choke him, and call him stupid. Terry shared how he was beaten with extension cords, high heels, and baseball bats, and pushed off a two-story building and into traffic, where he was hit by cars.

Miraculously, he survived, but he would still find himself regularly locked out of the family home and forced to face the cold Chicago winters alone, sleeping on porches and in abandoned basements. He would often rummage throughout the city, looking for food in garbage cans, eating whatever he could find. The scanty cardboard boxes he found for shelter barely kept him warm, but they kept him safe from the mammoth rats that tried to creep in. Despite what he faced, Terry always found a way back into the family home, where he endured even more trauma, from being sexually abused and violated, to having his head bashed against a radiator and knives and nails driven through his hands and feet.

As horrific as his ordeal was, things got worse when, at fourteen, he went with his mother and her boyfriend on a road trip. They drove all the way from Chicago to Mississippi, where they finally stopped and pushed him out of the car, discarding him like trash. He was left by the side of the road, dejected, rejected, and in despair. Although the abuse ended, his suffering continued, as Terry was eventually picked up by authorities in Mississippi, when he was found rummaging in a garbage can for food. When no adult would claim him, Terry was placed in foster care, in a group home for boys.

Terry slowly began to receive the support, guidance, and love that would nurture his soul and change the course of his life. People saw something special in him, and everywhere he went, teachers, social workers, and community leaders showed a keen interest in his development and progress. In high school, the administrators discovered that Terry was exceptionally gifted and intelligent, with an incredible memory. This led to him applying and being accepted into NASA's cooperative education program right after he graduated from high school.

From there, through hard work, perseverance, and the mentorship of the adults in his life, he went on the fast track to completing his master's degree in electrical engineering and being accepted into Massachusetts Institute of Technology. Eventually, Terry was able to obtain a doctoral degree from the University of Virginia and began to soar professionally and personally.

Instead of emotionally succumbing to the pain of his early rejection and allowing it to be a stumbling block for the rest of his life, Terry used his experience as a stepladder to bigger and better things. This choice helped to propel him from the cold and difficult streets of Chicago to such notable places as the White House and Pentagon, spreading his message of hope. In addition to his vast responsibilities as a research scientist, he travels throughout the nation, empowering others with his inspirational life story.[48] Dr. Morris encourages people to not let the circumstances of their rejection hinder the endless possibilities that can be afforded to all who desire, to live life abundantly in spite of adversity.

---

48   Chufo, Veronica. "Child abuse survivor talks about the road to recovery." DailyPress.com. May 17, 2011. http://www.dailypress.com/health/dp-nws-cp-child-abuse-recovery-20110517-story.html.

PRINCIPLE 4
RECALL—TESTIMONY

JESUS HEALS THE BLIND MAN

If you have ever been inside a courtroom, you may have noticed the finely-tuned legal orchestra that unfolds. Different parts are played by various people who use the instruments of their voice to ensure that justice is served. Enthusiastic lawyers advocate on behalf of their clients, while keen and observant juries waft through the dissonance, rhythmically listening to both sides until the tune crescendos with the judge's final disposition. Out of all the people in this ensemble, the witness makes the most noteworthy performance. With a wave of the baton, the spotlight falls on the eyewitness who takes center stage and provides an arrangement of their observations and experiences. Under the transformative power of their testimony, the witness has the ability to change lives forever. Many a case has been won or lost based on the credibility and performance of the star witness.

A prime example of this manifestation is the story of the blind man that Jesus heals in John 9:1-43. The blind man's testimony provides the solid evidence needed to win over a jury of his peers. The transition from bystander to witness remarkably captures how, after living in darkness, the blind man encounters the light source and gains the gift of sight. By testifying and sharing how he has triumphed over a life of rejection, the blind man gets people talking, bearing witness to the miraculous power of Christ.

As Jesus and His disciples journey in ministry throughout the land, Jesus serves as the Master of teachable moments, taking many opportunities to share life lessons with them. As they walk and talk, the disciples observe what appears to be a drifter sitting by the side of the road. When they get closer to him, it becomes obvious that he is visually impaired and destitute. Many times, in their quest for spiritual enlightenment, the disciples ask the Messiah thought-provoking questions. Wanting to prove to Jesus that they are astute pupils, they take the liberty to use this man's situation as a case study.

They ask Jesus, "Rabbi, who sinned, this man or his parents, that he was born blind?"[49] In asking this question, they think that they are crafty, and that their inquiry will prompt the Savior of the world to launch into a philosophical debate about the cause and effect of sin.

From the blind man's perspective, hearing them ask this question about his life, one can imagine that his interest is certainly piqued. For years, this man sat by the side of the dusty road, desperate for someone to acknowledge him, but he is used to being treated like a second-class citizen, people ignoring him or making unpleasant comments as they walk by. He can sense the contempt of the community, believing that his condition is self-inflicted. So, it must be an odd feeling to have these men stop and pay attention to him, but it isn't long before the blind man concludes that these men are just like everyone else.

He may be blind, but his hearing is impeccable, and in their voices, he hears and feels their hidden agenda. Instead of wanting to tend to his needs, they have the gall to try and dissect his life—not so that they can help him, but so they can boost their own egos. His senses are keen, and his ears perk up to hear the answer to the question that he has probably asked a million times.

---

49   John 9:2 NIV

Neither the blind man nor the disciples are prepared for the response that Jesus gives. Jesus answers, "Neither this man nor his parents sinned but this happened so that the works of God might be displayed in him."[50] With just a few words, the Messiah completely debunks the disciples' theory, and in the same breath encapsulates the blind man's entire life. *This happened so that the works of God might be displayed in him.*

The *this* that happens refers not only to his blindness but to all the years of rejection the man has experienced, the anguish from being cast aside, the shame from being different, and the turmoil from being forgotten. The magnitude of all he has been through is remarkably summed up by one simple word: *this.* At the time, the blind man cannot make sense of it all. Here he is, nondescript, disabled, and disregarded; how could the works of God possibly be displayed in him? How could all the misery and indifference he has experienced possibly be of some benefit to the kingdom? As this man's tale unfolds and is retold, he gains spiritual victory over his rejection, and miraculously receives much more than his sight.

* * *

NO TEST, NO TESTIMONY!

On the wall in my office is a large tattered picture frame that I've had for many years and refuse to throw away. The frame is nicked and scratched and the glass covering is cracked from when I dropped it moving into a new office. From time to time, I find myself staring at the picturesque scene of a magnified ripple effect from the splash of a rock being dropped in water. But it's the quote at the top of the frame that really captivates my attention and makes me never want to part with the old beat up picture frame. It reads: *Experience is a hard teacher. She gives the test first and the lesson afterwards.*

Such simple words, and yet a profound concept that places life's

---

50   John 9:3

journey into perspective. The quote reminds us that things will happen in life that may initially confound the mind and challenge us to the core. Only at the conclusion of the matter, when we come out on the other side, do we realize the purpose it held in our life. Yet, for some reason, this theory flies in the face of what we have been taught in school—that you get the lesson first, study hard, and then comes the test. In most of life's circumstances, this is not the case, and oftentimes you experience agonizing situations only to fully understand and value the outcome later on.

This sums up the life of the blind man; in his life, he receives the test first and the lesson afterwards. He first has to endure the trials of being physically handicapped and socially isolated, before he can experience and appreciate the lesson of deliverance through healing. What he recognizes after the fact, and what we should now learn, is that, on the one hand, there will always be a test, and on the other, there will be victory for those who endure to the end! Nobody likes a test, but they sure do love the reward that comes from passing the test.

There is good news, because if you have one, then you must have the other; if you have sorrow, you can have joy; if you have despair, you can have hope; if you have pain, you can have peace, and if you have darkness, you can experience God's miraculous light. Always remember that a test wrapped in the package of rejection can produce the gift of victory in Christ Jesus. Be encouraged, endure through the rigors and rigmarole of the test now, and then reap the rewards of overcoming later on.

After the disciples try to get all *philosophical* on the Great Philosopher with their ill-conceived analytical question, they are the ones left stunned and confounded by His response. Jesus does not have time to play juvenile games with the disciples, volleying the question of this man's life back and forth, debating or hypothesizing; the Lord refuses to have this man's life summarized in a round of the blame game when He has the cure.

Never one to mince His words, He speaks to them without filter, pronouncing that life's tests occur to produce a testimony, to illuminate the greatness of God! With those simple words, he moves forward and transforms the blind man's life. Jesus then spits on the ground, makes a poultice of mud, and puts it on the man's eyes, giving the blind man lifesaving instructions that will cleanse him externally and internally. "Go," he tells him, "wash in the Pool of Siloam"[51] (this word means "Sent"). So, the man goes and washes, and comes home seeing.

What an incredible lesson to learn—that sometimes, out of the nastiest stuff, deep down in the muck and mire of life experiences, evolves some of the most amazing and beautiful, insightful outcomes. Out of the darkest and dingiest of places, when interspersed with the essence of the Master, what splendor and awe we can behold. We must understand that even in the gloomiest of situations, God's hand can move, and while we still have time, there is work to be done so that others can see and follow the light. Praise God that the more you grow in Christ, the more you can see your trials and tests with renewed vision and spirit-filled perspective. Instead of shrinking away from these experiences, they should be seized, in order to help us evolve into Christ-perfected beings, always remembering that, if you let it, a test can bring about a powerful testimony.

* * *

GIVE `EM SOMETHING TO TALK ABOUT! INQUIRING MINDS WANT TO KNOW!

The blind man's encounter with Jesus and His disciples seems simple enough. They stop by the side of the road, the disciples ask a question, Jesus answers, gives the man instructions, the blind man obeys, and then goes on to live happily ever after. But that's not quite how the story goes, because things get even more complicated after he receives his sight. The man barely has time to enjoy his newfound

---

51   John 9:7

vision before he becomes embroiled in public controversy.

The blind man doesn't mean to stir the pot, but everywhere he goes, people talk about him. They stop, stare in amazement, and start talking about his transformation. They aren't quite sure if he is the same person they ignored and neglected all those years. For so long, he was a non-entity, and now, all of a sudden, he's the talk of the town. It's truly amazing what can happen in an encounter with Christ; you can instantly go from being nobody to somebody. People talk behind his back and in front of his face, asking questions, wondering what happened to him, perplexed when he no longer fits their preconceived notions and the box that they put him in.

This cause célèbre must be overwhelming for him, as he isn't used to people making a fuss over him, and now his very presence is making a ripple in the community and beyond. What is amazing is that, throughout the entire exchange with the disciples, Jesus, and his inquisitive neighbors, the story does not depict the blind man speaking. He is talked about, spoken to, and questioned, yet he never mumbles a word. Not until he can no longer stand the clamor of their chatter is his voice heard. Questions swirl about, over and over again: *who are you? What happened to you? Where is the blind man? Who did this to you?* He has enough of them digging into his life, and he finally opens his mouth and proclaims, "I am the man!"

His pronouncement, with its double meaning, speaks volumes—I am the man that was blind, but now I can see. I am the man laughed at and scorned, but now I am the man whose life has begun anew. I am the man who sat chained to the road, but now I am the man who has been set free; I am the man!

Instead of speculation, he proudly confirms who he is through his testimony. His acknowledgement of his past serves as a springboard, propelling him into who he is ordained to be in Jesus Christ. The people only see one side of him, through the lens of rejection, whereas with his sight, he sees himself in terms of the possibilities of a life touched by Christ.

* * *

GLORIFY GOD

It probably feels like being at a press conference, as question after question is thrown at the blind man, with demands for answers. Or maybe it feels like he is on trial, because even after he testifies, the crowds are not appeased, and they take him before the appellate court of the Pharisees. The situation turns into a spectacle that completely takes the focus away from where it belongs. The blind man has just experienced the most climatic moment of his life, but here, at this critical junction in his life, instead of being warmly embraced and doted on, this man is carried around the town as though he were a freak. For the first time in his life, all five of his senses are functioning, allowing him to have a full and complete experience. Finally, he can taste and see the water as he washes in the pool of Siloam. Now, he can hear and see the children as they laugh and play around him. At last, he can put a face to voices he has heard so many times as they swished past, overlooking him in the heat of the day.

Yet his first human contact after gaining his sight is not that of welcoming faces, but of perplexed curiosity and disbelief. He may already have a hunch about their apathy, but now he confirms it with his very own eyes. The sad part of this story is that the Pharisees, so-called spiritual leaders of the community, the ones deemed to be closest to God, don't even recognize the miracle in front of them. Instead, they too pepper him with questions that are irrelevant compared to the change in this man's life.

Astonishingly, they aren't making this big fuss about his situation so that they, too, can tap into the power of his healing; they do so out of condemnation. This man's testimony grabs their attention, but they choose to see it in a negative light. The more they try to understand and conceptualize the occurrence, the further they move away from the truth. They get caught up on the legalities surrounding the man's healing instead of seeing the bigger picture. As a result, they miss the opportunity to partake in the miracle and obtain healing for themselves and others.

Every minute detail of Christ's journey on earth is purposeful, accompanied by a lesson plan for us to learn. When Jesus gives specific instructions to the blind man, telling him to go to the pool of Siloam and wash in it, His message begins to unfold. Initially, the rationale behind this directive is not clear. Why does Jesus specifically tell the man to wash in the pool of Siloam? Does it have some miraculous healing nutrients that no one knows about? What is so significant about this particular pool of water? The Lord could have sent him to any pool in the region or, even better, God Almighty could have healed the man right there on the spot. Do Christ's instructions to go to this specific pool have some latent meaning that needed to be uncovered?

The answer to these questions just may rest in the name of the pool: *Siloam*. By examining the word, we can understand the rationale behind the Messiah's directive to the blind man. The word *Siloam* is the Greek transliteration of the Hebrew name *Shiloah*, which comes from the Hebrew verb *shalah*, which means "to send out or *let go*." It's most frequently used to describe the action of one person who sends another person somewhere or to do something and frequently describes God sending someone on a journey.[52]

Some contemporary dictionaries define *to send* or *send out* as dispatching someone on an errand or to convey a message. With this newfound meaning, we begin to see that Jesus strategically tells the blind man to go to the pool of Siloam, with the hopes of conveying a multilayered, object lesson. The pool of Siloam in and of itself does not have any miraculous healing powers or sight-giving nutrients; otherwise, people would have been flocking to it a long time ago for its restorative powers. It is just an ordinary pool that

---

52   Abarim Publications. "Siloam Meaning." Accessed September 15, 2016. http://www.abarim-publications.com/Meaning/Siloam.html#.Vwa-Kf72bcs

people use to fetch water, to sustain their families and care for their personal needs.

When the blind man obeys Christ's instructions and completes his journey to the Pool of Siloam, that is when he truly receives his sight. Jesus sends him there for the sole purpose of experiencing the benefits of obedience. When the blind man follows these instructions, the life of rejection he has experienced is washed away, and replaced with a testimony that makes waves in his community and beyond.

The Lord sends the blind man to the Pool of Siloam so that we can learn that our experience with rejection, listening to His directives, our subsequent obedience, and healing and testimony, are all intricately interlinked. The blind man is directed to complete an act, and that one feat changes his life and propels him into a living, breathing, walking testimony. The Lord *sent* the blind man to a pool called *Sent*, and as he becomes one with the pool, he becomes *sent*, to share his testimony with others. No longer is his identity bound in his rejection, but has now become his testimony.

Born into sin, we are like the blind man, aimlessly sitting by the road of life, desperate for someone to rescue and instruct us how to overcome the rejection that has sidelined us. In the midst of the fray, the Master will always stop by, and if you are willing to be healed, God will send you on a journey of a lifetime. Through the power of Jesus Christ, your testimony can give sight to the blind, let the deaf hear, heal those who are infirm, and transform and save those who don't even know that they are dying.

No matter what you do, people are going to talk about you, so why not let it be about the amazing testimony of a life in Jesus Christ? Don't hold back your story because of fear. Remember that it's the outcome that matters the most; you have a part in scripting your story and designing what your future should look like. You must stop hiding or running from our story, and instead confirm it, be bold about it, embrace who God has allowed you to be. Each time you share your testimony, you affirm God's transformative power in your life and quell the noise of your detractors and naysayers. Be proud of where God has brought you, and revel in a blessed future instead of living in rejection's past. Share who you are and what you have been through, while boldly proclaiming who you are now and where you are going.

Our tests help to produce our testimony, and the sharing of this experience helps to confirm God's wondrous working power. So powerful is the work of testifying that, thousands of years later, we are still talking about the testimonies of courageous men and women whom God used, in the most challenging situations, to manifest His glory. Amazing stories such as Esther's courage in the midst of a death sentence, Daniel's unwavering faith in the lion's den, and Job's triumph through tragedy continue to testify of God's goodness and mercy. Our testimony of deliverance is no different than theirs, and when told, it can have the same long-lasting impact today as in the days of old.

As ambassadors of Jesus Christ, you become an evangelist, proclaiming your story of triumph and deliverance to all who will hear. As champions for Christ, your testimony is the jersey you wear that signifies which team you are on. The bumps, bruises, and scars garnered on the field in the form of tests, trials, and rejection are medals of honor, revealing the story of your triumph and victory. We each have a choice to share our testimony or conceal it, but through sharing, true faith, obedience, and success occur.

Like the Pharisees who refuse to hear the truth of the blind man's testimony, when we share our story of deliverance with others, what is done with this information is left up to those who have heard—they are accountable for every testimony they have received. The blind man's experience with Jesus turns his life of rejection into a powerful testimony. Likewise, you are commissioned to share your story and seize the opportunity to impact lives with your experience of triumph over adversity.

PRINCIPLE 4: RECALL—TESTIMONY

REJECTION CREATES THE OPPORTUNITY FOR US TO
SHARE WITH OTHERS OUR TESTIMONY IN OVERCOMING,
AND FOR JESUS TO DEMONSTRATE VICTORY THROUGH HIM.

1. Did my rejection experience give me a testimony
   that I can share with others?

   _____

   _____

   _____

2. Am I experiencing this rejection because God is
   using this situation to show His power and divinity,
   give hope, and to reach and save others?

   _____

   _____

   _____

3. Can my testimony help encourage and empower
   someone?

   _____

   _____

   _____

4. Would sharing my testimony help me to heal?

   _____

   _____

   _____

TESTIMONY FIVE:

MY DISAPPOINTMENT, HIS APPOINTMENT

Sometimes, the rejection you face can occur because there is a divine appointment waiting on the other side that God wants you to keep. The Lord masterfully coordinates your position in life, and a U-turn is often the direct result of God maneuvering you to effect the most change, bringing souls closer to establishing a relationship with Christ. We should remember that divine appointments are more important than any rejection we may face.

I recall during my early social work years, when I was feeling burnt out and applying for various jobs within the agency, that there was a young lady in the same unit as I, and we both applied and got interviews for the same position. I was informed later that I didn't get the job and that she was chosen as the better candidate instead. I was disappointed that I didn't get the job, and frustrated with God for not answering my prayers. In spite of how I was feeling, the Holy Spirit nudged me to call the young lady who got the job and congratulate her.

Still stinging from the rejection, I went back and forth about whether or not I should call. Finally, out of obedience, I humbled myself and called the young lady, congratulating her on getting the job and wishing her well in this new career opportunity. She shared with me that she was nervous about how I would react, wondering if I would be upset with her. I reassured her that I was pleased about her promotion and looked forward to seeing her grow professionally. She said that she was relieved, and we chatted for a few more minutes before ending the phone call.

This gesture paved the way for us to get to know each other better, and a friendship developed. Months later, I invited her to a Bible study that a local elder was hosting for some of my co-workers. She eagerly came to every meeting, examined and studied the Word, and eventually accepted the Lord Jesus Christ as her Savior, and was baptized into the faith. Several months later, through her example, her mother was baptized, and then years later, her young daughter accepted the message of Christ and was also baptized.

This young lady is now considered one of my dearest friends, and she is a godmother to our daughter. My soul rejoices, and I walk away from this experience with a renewed sense of understanding and gratefulness to the Lord. I realize now why the Lord did not allow me to get the job. It was a two-fold lesson for the both of us. For me, it was an exercise in humility, and for her, a demonstration of Godly graciousness. This divine appointment in a simple congratulatory phone call mushroomed into a special friendship where I could witness to her about God's truth and faithfulness. I cringe to think about what would've happened if I disobeyed and had a nasty attitude with her, mistreating her after she got the job that I wanted. If I had gotten the job, we may not have connected the way we did, and maybe, *just maybe*, she would not have had another opportunity to be introduced to Christ.

While I don't know what would've happened if another scenario played out, in hindsight I am ever grateful to God for allowing me to keep this divine appointment with rejection. This door closing enabled me to focus on a realm outside of myself, with the realization that everything is not about me! With this newfound perspective, I recognize that what we go through in life, whether good or bad, should bring us and, most importantly, those around us, ever closer to God.

Principle 5
Rejoice—Worship

Paul and Silas

"In everything give thanks; for this is God's will for you in Christ Jesus."[53]

At first glance, this text seems simple enough. The reader is encouraged to have a heart of thankfulness and be grateful for the many blessings that the Lord bestows. With love in our hearts for our families, friends, a job, and a roof over our head, it is not hard to lift up our voices for the goodness and mercy God showers upon us each new day. However, in the context of rejection, this scripture encouraging us to give thanks in *everything* almost seems like an oxymoron. How are you supposed to open your mouth to give praise and thanks when you're faced with a mountain of rejection? Does the Lord really expect you to give thanks when your heart is heavy and filled with pain?

Many times, we get so caught up in our story of hurt—the bad from our dad and the trauma from ya momma—that we neglect to see the handiwork of the Lord in the midst of what we are going through. The hurt from the rejection is so all-consuming that, at that very moment, we can only see life through the lens of pain-filled eyes; so much so that everything we do, say, and see is viewed only

---

53   1 Thess. 5:18 KJV

in relation to the rejection and hurt we've experienced. Oftentimes, we in turn use our experience to inflict pain and rejection on others, with the belief that, if we are experiencing emotional pain, then so should everyone we come in contact with. We wield our pain like a weapon and use our circumstances as a crutch. Instead, we should use the moment as a golden opportunity to realize that, in spite of it all, you should thank God that you are alive! Yes, if you're alive, you will feel pain and rejection—this is a direct result of sin. As believers of Christ, we are not exempt from the ramifications of sin; this is not high school, where if you have excelled throughout the school year, the teacher exempts you from the final exam.

"For he maketh His sun to rise on the evil and on the good, and sendeth rain on the just and on the unjust."[54] No, we are not excused. As inhabitants of the earth, we will feel the effects of sin, and sin brings about pain, rejection, and suffering. But the Lord, in His infinite wisdom, does not want His children to remain beleaguered in this state for too long, because it would suffocate and stifle our ability to grow in Him. The Lord provides His children with a defense mechanism—the elements of worship, reflective rejoicing, and perpetual thankfulness can overturn the fervent attempts of rejection to stymie our Christian growth.

There is a reason God's word urges us to *give thanks* and rejoice in the Lord always. The Lord knows that sin weighs us down. God strategically placed this remarkable advice and golden nugget in His word—*in everything give thanks*—because psychologically and physiologically, there is power in shifting your mind-frame from the negative to the positive. The very act of being thankful releases potent chemicals and endorphins within the body, which enable you to see a painful and hopeless situation in a better light. Reflecting on the things that you have to be thankful for can far outweigh and surpass any rejection or pain you are going through, eventually changing the outlook of your situation. Making thankfulness a daily

---

54   Matt. 5:45

part of your worship enables your muscles of gratitude to grow and strengthens you. The Word of God is saying, in every situation, find something, anything, to be thankful for.

Giving thanks is interchangeable with worship. Through our worship, we express how truly thankful we are, and in giving thanks to the Master, we worship Him. No one exemplifies the true merits of thankfulness and worship more so than Paul and Silas. These two preachers could be poster boys for the power of turning rejection into rejoicing. Their story unveils the resiliency of a Christ-filled spirit even in the direst of circumstances.

*   *   *

INNOCENT

As dedicated colleagues of faith, Paul and Silas travel throughout the land preaching deliverance. They bring hope and healing to those who are suffering and help to set people on a path to freedom in Christ. However, before Paul is delivered and transformed with love, he is filled with all-consuming hatred for those who do not believe as he does. Paul is initially considered a zealot and persecutor, who makes it his life's mission to hunt and annihilate people who dare to contradict his strict religious beliefs. His staunch worldview gives way to bitterness and anger, and for many years he stands as the evil rejecter of Christ's followers, and under his authority, numerous Christians are tortured and brutally murdered.

Thankfully, on the road to Damascus, Paul has a life-changing encounter with God that revolutionizes and transforms his way of thinking and being in the world. On this dusty road, Paul meets the Savior and receives salvation. Now, instead of rejecting people, he embraces them into a life of redemption, genuine acceptance, and love, through Christ Jesus.

With this newfound freedom, Paul, later joined by his loyal companion, Silas, travels to and fro, sharing the good news.

Throughout their travels, they run into many different people and face countless obstacles and challenges. In a chance encounter with one particular woman, through no fault of their own, they find themselves locked up in jail, facing the bitter wall of rejection. In Acts 16, a woman in the community who is possessed with evil spirits tells fortunes, and in doing so, she makes her handlers lots of money. She goes throughout town, allegedly forecasting community members lives and, for a hefty price, people who hunger to know their future can hear her foolishness. This scheme nets her handlers a significant nest egg, and they will do anything to ensure that she continues on this path.

As she comes upon Paul and Silas, her unclean spirit is overpowered by the Holy Spirit within them, and she cries out, repetitively, "These men are servants of the Most High God, who are telling you the way to be saved."[55] She cannot stop herself from prophesying, and she continuously blurts out that they are men of God. On first impression, it may seem as though this woman has good intentions, is enthralled with their spirit, and wants to share in their message of truth. However, Paul and Silas know better; she stands in close proximity to them, yelling out this claim, as a way of mocking God and trivializing their assignment. Manipulated by the enemy for wicked gain, this woman overshadows Paul and Silas with her shenanigans, diverting others from truly seeing the purpose of their visit. If she continues along in this manner, then Paul and Silas will surely lose their effectiveness in the community, and no one will be drawn to them as long as they were associated with her demonic spirit.

How on earth can Paul's voice of liberation stand out amid the cacophony of her deceptive shrill? Even though they try to ignore her, she continues on, until her chant reaches a fevered and aggravating pitch. Paul, annoyed with the incessant vocalizing, looks beyond her and into what controls her. He recognizes that the "struggle

---

55   Acts 16:17 NIV

is not against flesh and blood, but against the rulers, against the authorities, against the powers of this dark world and against the spiritual forces of evil in the heavenly realms."[56]

Holding these principles in mind, Paul takes action, and with the authority of God's kingdom, he speaks the powerful words that make every demon tremble and flee: "In the name of Jesus Christ I command you to come out of her!"[57] In a single, monumental sentence, the demons that hold this woman captive are rendered useless, devoid of any further control over her life. While the Word does not say what happens to this woman after she is delivered from the demons, one can imagine that the rejection she experienced for all of those years vanishes in an instant and no longer matters, because she is now free and set on a path towards acceptance.

No longer can she be used as a puppet for financial gain; she is of no use to her earthly masters, who seethe with anger, as their investment no longer yields the dividends they desire. Her handlers divert their attention to Paul and Silas, bent on retribution and revenge for the perceived destruction of their venture capital. While this woman is now loosed from the chains that bound her, the complete opposite becomes the fate of these two prophets. Even though what Paul and Silas do is actually a good thing, their genuine intentions are taken for bad, and they are swiftly brought before the authorities so that justice can be meted out.

If these handlers moved that fast to get this woman help when the demons clouded her brain, this story may have turned out much different. People who do not even know the prophets join in chorus with the woman's handlers, demanding that they be persecuted and imprisoned. Paul and Silas are captured, severely beaten, brutally tortured, thrown into prison, and shackled to a wall, and they have done absolutely nothing wrong! What a predicament—innocent yet guilty, and rejected by the very same community they have come to

---

56   Eph. 6:12

57   Acts 16:18

help save. How does the God that sent them permit such horrific things to happen in His name? Where is the justice? As the story unfolds, their worship looses the shackles of rejection that bind them.

* * *

MIDNIGHT PRAISE BREAK

By the time their attackers are finished with them, Paul and Silas look like a wreck. Covered in welts, with blood seeping from multiple contusions, they are in excruciating pain and quite possibly in and out of consciousness. At that moment, they are considered public enemy number one, and the directives given to the guard on duty are for him to treat them as such. The guard takes his job very seriously, and to ensure their security, he places them in the innermost section of the jail. This strategy is put in place in the hopes of thwarting any supernatural attempts at escape. The guard's hypervigilance is well warranted—after all, these prisoners are the very same ones who, with a single sentence, cast demons out of a woman. Surely they can take this same skill-set and flee the confines of this labyrinth.

So, as Paul and Silas sit, indefatigable, in the dank and dark prison cell, they don't know who is around them, but they smell the stench of suffering and the plight of desperation in the air. The innermost part of the prison is not only the securest area but also the darkest part, with no light anywhere to seep through. For these men, the less light they physically see, the more reliant they are on the marvelous light of Jesus, the light of the world.

The Bible states that, at about midnight, Paul and Silas are praying and singing hymns to God.[58] There is something about midnight, the dawning of a new day, that can transfix or transform the soul. Midnight is typically the darkest part in a twenty-four-hour period, and it is also when people who are ill or have a fever tend to

---

58 Acts 16:25

take a turn for the worse or the better. A high level of significance and symbolism is attributed to this time of day, as it indicates the passing of the old and progressing with the new.

Paul and Silas are not sure what fate lies ahead of them, and based on the day's events, their forecast looks grim. Stripped of their belongings, innocence, and mission, they could sit there and rehash their plight, unsure of what the next day will bring. Amazingly, at the darkest hour, Paul and Silas choose to bring forth the only thing they have left—something that no chain, prison guard or penitentiary fortress can stop—*their worship*. Physically bruised and battered, and emotionally rejected at their lowest point, Paul and Silas sit in the dark, invisible to each other, yet still attuned to the calming comfort of the Holy Spirit, and they worship.

The Word is not clear on who starts the praise and worship session. Is it Silas, who, in spite of his perturbation, as a faithful and loyal companion to Paul sings songs to God in encouragement to his friend? Or is it Paul, seasoned and assured in his faith, embodying Job's principle: "though he slay me, yet will I trust in Him."[59] Instead of drowning in the perplexities of their situation, they make the salient choice to have a praise break, a pause from the cruel intentions of the world, elevating them to loftier heights than any man can restrain. While they are physically detained by the antics of men, mentally they lie prostrate, through their worship, freeing their spirits to praise God in tandem with powerful petitions and celestial songs.

For the most part, when someone is assaulted in the manner Paul and Silas are, survival mode kicks in, necessitating self-preservation. The natural inclination is to curl up tight in the fetal position. At such a critical time, to sing and pray might be considered, by some, to be an unnatural thing to do. The act of praise and worship is an external expression of internal spiritual ruminations. Something on the inside has to propel the believer to demonstrate what is at the

---

59   Job 13:15 KJV

core of their being. In Paul and Silas' case, while their physical beings are sorely depleted, their spiritual beings gain stamina and strength through sacrificial veneration. Their decision to have a midnight praise break at the most challenging hour of their lives speaks volumes about the power of the mind over physical wellbeing.

Every rejected believer must choose to praise and worship to the highest state when they are low. Paul and Silas set an example for all to follow, because at their most vulnerable, they expose themselves to the Sustainer, and in doing so, fresh new life is bestowed upon them.

Paul and Silas can choose to either worship or stew in their current troubles. One option will bring them closer to genuine freedom, and the other will keep them emotionally and physically confined. With their choice clear, Paul and Silas transition from prisoners to praisers, deferring to their one and only Master. Their fellow inmates are in awe of the mellifluous sounds standing in stark contrast to the prison clamor that usually fills the dank environment. From inmates banging on the metal bars of their cell, to the weeping and groaning of men in physical and mental anguish, to the jangle of chains rattling as the prisoners attempt to move about, each sound clashes with the songs of hallelujah that permeate the air.

It is not clear which hymns they sing. Are they melancholy hymns of woe, or are they songs of joy and hope? Regardless of the theme, each song points to a Savior, who can abundantly exceed all that they can ever ask. The prisoners' ears perk up, possibly at the rhythmic tones or the divine lyrics, poetically juxtaposed, capturing their attention. All other sounds cease—a meditative mood settles in as the most wretched of prisoners stand still and respectful, tears streaming down some of their faces, quite possibly flashing back to childhood melodies that their mothers sang.

No longer do they wince and whine from emotional and physical pain; the prayers and psalms of the righteous serve as a salve to the wounded prisoner's soul. Broken, yet trans-fixed in worship, the timbre from their voices reaches a fevered pitch at the exact same time as a jarring rumble disrupts their zealous song service. The One who created the heaven and the earth shakes the foundations upon which they lie, causing a mighty earthquake. Not sure what is going on, the prisoners are probably fearful, wondering if the rocks from the prison walls will fall, killing them all. Paul and Silas know that their situation can get no worse and quite possibly raise their voices even louder, ringing out in chorus, "Never will the rocks cry out in my place, He's worthy of all my praise."[60]

Sediment from the earth stirs up in their cells, blinding the prisoners as they brace for the walls to cave in. As quickly as the earthquake begins, it ends. As their senses slowly come back to them, they touch their skin, noting that they have no bruises, broken bones, or wounds from the mighty earthquake. The men blink, astonished that they are still alive, and even more incredulous that they are now unencumbered. Miraculously, the earthquake not only leaves them unscathed, but the chains that confined them are now loosed, and the doors to their cells swing open.

Interestingly enough, not all of these men are innocent like Paul and Silas, thrown behind bars for a crime they did not commit. Some of these men deserve to be locked up, with the key to the jailhouse thrown away, for their good and the betterment of others. However, for whatever merciful reasons, a force greater than any crime these prisoners may have committed deems it fit that they be free, not because they are worthy, but as a demonstration of the outcome of worship. Even more astonishing: in spite of the wide-open passage to freedom before them, each prisoner remains in place.

It's not clear how the guard sleeps through this chain of events, or whether the mighty force of the earthquake renders him unconscious, but as the dust settles, he arises, perplexed and discombobulated. The last thing he remembers is sounds of psalms and praise emanating from the maximum-security cell block. As

---

60   McClendon, Bishop Clarence. "I Came to Magnify the Lord." *Shout Hallelujah.* Sony, 2000.

he comes to his senses, the worst thing that could ever happen to a prison guard unfolds before his eyes. Cell doors open in any prison setting is never a good sign, and signals disastrous consequences for him and those he is there to protect. Like a good soldier, the guard is taught to follow orders, and when these new prisoners, Paul and Silas, are placed under his supervision, special instructions are given to ensure their confinement and not let them out of his sight. To even consider that they could be gone brings dread to his mind as he imagines his fate at the discovery of loose criminals out of the jail, all on his watch.

The only solution he can visualize is to take his own life, to preempt the trouble he will find himself in because of this catastrophic situation. Thankfully, salvation trumps death, as Paul urgently intervenes, revealing the enormity of the miracle—not one prisoner has escaped. The guard tasked with keeping them restrained is now freed by those he keeps prisoner. In an instant, the guard is given a transformative lease on life, not because of anything that he does, but because of the example set by Paul and Silas at the worst time in their lives. Their obedience, worship, and offerings of praise provide the ticket to God's favor, not only for the singers, but for all who bear witness to their situation. The guard hungers for what they have, and their demonstration opens the gateway for him and his entire family to receive salvation.

Paul and Silas experience rejection, not through any fault of their own, but to serve as a catalyst for the redemption and salvation of others. Even though they are innocent, if they don't go through the hardship of being brutally beaten, locked away, and having their rights stripped from them, then the prisoners, the guard, and his entire household might not have the opportunity to receive the benefits of worship.

By holding firm to God, trusting and believing, knowing that eventually a good outcome will manifest that will far surpass the bad experiences, your worship gains the attention of others and can even set free those who don't know that they are enslaved. Lifting up the name of the Lord in the midst of rejection always allows God's glory to be shown in ways that you could not even imagine.

PRINCIPLE 5: REJOICE—WORSHIP

THE WORD OF GOD SAYS, "IN ALL THINGS GIVE THANKS";
THEREFORE, EVEN IN THE MIDST OF YOUR REJECTION
EXPERIENCE, GIVE GOD GLORY AND WORSHIP HIM.

1. Even though I may not understand what I am going
    through, do I really believe that God works all things
    for the good of those who love Him?

    _____

    _____

    _____

2. Can I consistently trust and worship God even
    though I still have not received my breakthrough in
    this situation?

    _____

    _____

    _____

3. Can my approach to worshipping God intercede and free someone else?

_____

_____

_____

4. Can my response to rejection through worship dictate the outcome of what appears to be a no-win situation?

_____

_____

_____

REJECTION'S CHOICE

THE 13ᵀᴴ DISCIPLE— IT'S NOT OVER YET!

WHAT SHOULD WE DO NOW?

The story chronicled in Acts 1 details how the disciples' Master, Leader and Brother is horrifically executed, suffering a brutal death. The disciples experience the greatest loss of their lives. Although they have been forewarned, the pain is no less great. The crucifixion of Jesus devastates these normally austere men. As tears sting their faces and air painfully enters their lungs with each shallow breath, their heads pound with the reality that He is gone.

Reflections of their journey with Him loom large, from the feeding of the five thousand, to the faith-filled demonstration of walking on water, to healing, preaching, and teaching multitudes, Jesus always took the lead. The men, accustomed to Jesus' leadership, are stifled by uncertainty. What will happen next? What will become of them, and how will they go on without Him?

After the customary days of mourning, what remains of this distressed group travel to Jerusalem in search of what life will bring. At their destination, the eleven disciples huddle together for comfort, along with Mary, Jesus' mother, and several other women. A call for worship rings out, and more than a hundred mourners and sympathizers gather around the disciples and call upon the

Lord. As they lift their eyes heavenward, all they can do is pray. They know that they should not be anxious about anything, but in every situation, by prayer and petition, with thanksgiving, present their requests before God.[61]

As is often the case, this season of prayer provides clarity and lifts the cloud of grief, paving the way for restoration and future planning. Their shock, denial, and hurt turns to acceptance and motivation under the influence of God imploring them to rise up and continue the Master's legacy. With this renewed perspective, they attempt to reorganize and create a strategic plan.

Peter, self-appointed chairman, takes the lead and addresses the crowd, summarizing the current situation, offering words of encouragement, and touching on the betrayal of Judas. The disciples and those gathered feel the sting of Judas' deception. While prophecy foretold this treachery and the horrendous death of Jesus, it hurts no less to see it all come to pass. Judas was a part of them; he slept, ate, and talked with them, sitting at the feet of Jesus, learning the testaments of God's love. Judas, just like all of the other disciples, played an important role in Jesus' ministry on earth.

* * *

THE JOB OF A LIFETIME!

Despite Judas' disloyalty, his absence leaves a void that needs to be filled. Peter recommends that someone take Judas' place, extending the invitation for a new leader to join them on their quest to fulfill Jesus' creed. The disciples are skeptical at having to trust a new face. While some may inwardly question the need to add someone else to the team, their fears are alleviated. Clear guidelines are provided regarding where this newly-sought leader will come from. He will be someone from within their ranks, who traveled and labored in the vineyard with them, behind Jesus. Peace

---

61   Phil. 4:6 NIV

of mind settles in, as this means the person will not need much of an orientation.

Only two men meet the qualifications—Joseph Barsabas and Matthias. As candidates, you cannot find a better duo. They are just as dedicated and committed to the cause of Christ as the other eleven disciples. They long ago set aside the will to do their own thing, choosing instead to follow Jesus as He ministered on earth. It must be an exciting and anxious time for both men, wondering who will be the chosen one for this position of a lifetime. Here the opportunity is being presented for one of them to become a disciple, a soldier on the front lines, heralding the greatest story ever told. Whoever is chosen will go down in the annals of history as one of the great men responsible for sharing news of the most precious treasure ever given to mankind, the gift of salvation. While both men are equally equipped and eager to fulfill the task at hand, there is room for only one to be selected.

The disciples find themselves in quite a dilemma. From the outside, the candidates are equal in stature and presentation. Joseph and Matthias both demonstrate loyalty, faithfulness, and exemplary leadership skills, not to mention exhibiting high levels of motivation to teach and proclaim the love of Christ wherever they go. Peter and the rest of the men know that this decision cannot be made lightly, and because of this, they dare not trust in their own intuition.

It's quite possible the disciples remember a story from the days of old, when a similar situation occurred. The Lord sent Samuel[62] to seek out and anoint a replacement for Saul's waning leadership, and the best candidate had to be chosen. Jesse had several sons and God told Samuel that one of them would be king. As Samuel began this remarkable task, for whatever reason he thought that the very first son he laid eyes on fit the profile of what a king should look like. However, the Lord quickly put Samuel in his place with the caveat "Look not on his countenance, or on the height of his stature;

---

62   1 Sam. 16

because I have refused him: for the LORD seeth not as man seeth; for man looketh on the outward appearance, but the LORD looketh on the heart."[63]

The Word is clear: despite man's meticulous examination, what man can behold is only the *tip of the iceberg*.

Subsequently, like Samuel, the disciples can only assess Joseph and Matthias from a certain vantage point, but God the Creator can see beyond the depths of man's purview. Acknowledging their limitations, and to ensure that the decision is Holy-Spirit-led, the disciples' only recourse is to pray. A simple yet profound petition is made to the omniscient God: "Lord, you know everyone's heart. Show us which of these two you have chosen."[64] In addition to their prayer, to ensure that their biases and human inclinations do not influence the decision, they add another layer of surety by casting lots. According to ancient Judeo-Christian customs, *cleromancy*, the act of casting of lots, is a means by which God communicates with His followers. Comparable to the modern-day practice of drawing straws or rolling dice, the disciples use this systematic yet random process of elimination to discern the definitive will of God.

The disciples undoubtedly know that, though the lot is cast into the lap, its every decision is from the Lord.[65] They pray and cast lots between Joseph and Matthias, confident that whomever the lot falls upon is divinely selected to replace Judas. The moment of truth arrives, and the one chosen to carry the gospel mantle is none other than Matthias.

* * *

---

63   1 Sam. 16:7 KJV

64   Acts 1:24 NIV

65   Prov. 16:33

THE 13TH DISCIPLE

All around, people cheer and gather close to congratulate Matthias on joining the disciples at such a pivotal time in the organization's structure. The match-up between him and Joseph is exceptionally close, but the Lord designates Matthias to officially join the band of leadership, extolling the second coming. Matthias, whose name means *gift of God*, is given the ultimate gift, as many are called, but few are chosen.[66] What joy he must feel to be set apart for such mighty work.

Joseph, on the other hand, experiences the biggest rejection of his life. He too is grieving after all of these years with the Master, soaking up His love and instructions. His sorrow turns to hope at the thought that he is considered worthy to stand among these spiritual giants. His nickname, "Justus the Righteous One," is a good indication of his character and worthiness. Out of all the men that walked with Jesus, to be on the cusp of such a climactic occurrence is in itself miraculous, and Joseph eagerly awaits the outcome of the decision, only to find out that it isn't going to be him. With this crushing news, Joseph is probably swinging on a pendulum of emotions—from the high of being a candidate to the low of being eliminated, the perplexities he experiences may be too great to bear.

His confidence shaken, Joseph the *almost* disciple has to be in shock. Now he stands in front of the throng, bewildered at what went wrong. Waves of embarrassment crash over him as he processes the outcome, wondering what the people must be thinking of him. Many questions linger about how to deal with such a monumental let down. Do they think something is wrong with him? After all, God knows the heart, yet Joseph's heart seemingly isn't good enough for the job. Is there a spot, blemish, or wrinkle that precludes him from such an auspicious role? Does Joseph minimize Matthias' leadership skills, skeptical about the contribution Matthias can make to the

---

66   Matt. 22:14 NLT

gospel? Does Joseph exhibit a Luciferian spirit and turn against God, certain that the Lord made the wrong decision? Or does he humbly submit to divine authority, accepting the Lord's will? Does he agree with the decision, seeking to continue on the journey with the disciples? Does he swallow his pride and vow to follow in the footsteps of Jesus, affirming the gospel news each step of the way?

For some reason, the Bible does not depict what happens to Joseph after this event, so we don't know how his life pans out after the doors close on this opportunity. In spite of the fact that Joseph isn't able to make a noteworthy contribution with the disciples, his story still has great influence centuries later. There are powerful lessons to learn from Joseph that can teach us how to cope with rejection.

The first is that, like Joseph, we will all at some point have an encounter where a door we want to open will be closed to us. We should not be in denial, believing that rejection only occurs to other people; this is a fallacy. Rejection does not discriminate based on pedigree, gender, socioeconomic status, or any other societal distinction. From the most acclaimed to the meekest among us, the scenario is not *if* it will happen, but *when*. What you will experience is part of the normal cycle of life. The faster you recognize it for the teaching moment that it is, the better your outcome and recovery will be. Secondly, and the most important lesson of all, is the choice we make in response to the rejection we face. One thing is certain—Joseph makes a choice on how to deal with his experience.

Likewise, each of us will decide how to respond to that door being shut in our face. This choice will dictate the path we take in life, whether it is to our good or bad. The choice we make can draw us closer to Christ or put a wall between us and a loving merciful Savior. Every experience should be met with prayerful contemplation, yielding to the will of God. Take the time to reflect and analyze your situation by applying these principles and determining to learn and grow from the experience. Most importantly, search diligently and find a reason to rejoice, cultivating an attitude of worship, even in the most challenging circumstances. On earth, we may not get the answers we seek for why certain things have happened to us; however, if we persevere through faith, when we get to heaven, we will see with our own eyes the beautiful tapestry woven by the endurance and testimony of the saints. It will all be worthwhile.

So, what are you going to do when rejection comes knocking at your door? The choice now is up to you!

* * *

IT'S NOT OVER YET

A Chinese parable tells of a rural family long ago. The family has a horse that helps to plow the land and raise their food. One day, the horse runs away while the farmer's son is plowing the field.

Neighbors come and say to the old man and the boy, "We heard about your bad luck. It is so bad."

"How do you know it is bad?" answers the farmer. "It is not over yet!" Sure enough, in a few days the horse comes back, leading a herd of wild horses.

"We heard about your good luck and came to congratulate you," say the neighbors.

"How do you know it is good luck?" answers the farmer, "It is not over yet!" A few days later, while the boy is trying to train one of the horses, it throws him and breaks his leg.

"Oh," said the neighbors. "We heard about your bad luck and came to sympathize."

Again the old man replies, "How do you know it is bad? It is not over yet."

The parable ends by saying that a great war comes, and all of the able-bodied young men are taken off to fight. Most of them are killed in battle, but the boy with the broken leg stays at home and cares for his aging father for the rest of his days.

The moral of the story is that, even though your situation is questionable, things may not always be as they appear. While the rejection we experience in life may be overwhelming, God has an amazing way of turning things around. When we overcome and contrast these challenges with life lived eternally, every rejection will seem infinitesimal. You may not have control over how rejection impacts you, but you have control over how you respond. God has a master plan, and it is supremely better than any rejection we face, and we praise Him that His plan for our lives is not over yet!

APPENDIX

BONUS: STRANGE METHOD

In August 2010, the plight of thirty-three Chilean miners grabbed the attention of the world, as they lay submerged thousands of feet beneath a collapsed mine shaft in the Atacama Desert. No one above ground knew if the men were dead or alive, or if efforts would be focused on rescue or recovery. Thankfully, despair turned to hope as, seventeen days after the mine fell apart, ground was broken to reveal that all of the men were still alive.

It was a miracle that they had survived so long—with very little food, humid conditions, and cramped quarters, the odds were against them. A multi-nation coordinated effort was made to rescue these brave men, who were running out of time. Tireless manpower and unyielding machinery worked feverishly around the clock, drilling holes into the ground to send supplies to the men. Rescue organizers and government officials strategized scenarios to develop a plan to safely extricate the men. Time was against them; each day the men remained below, conditions worsened, and the risk for further collapse was alarmingly high.

A consensus determined that each man would be fit into a special container and cautiously lifted to the surface through one of the holes they had dug. Each man had to meet a size requirement to fit in the capsule and get through the escape tunnel. If they were not able to fit, they could not be transported above ground, and their rescue would be significantly delayed, with their lives in the balance. The Fenix capsule enclosure was twenty-eight inches in diameter and designed to fit and carry one person at a time. In order to fit into the Fenix capsule and be elevated above ground, the miners were put on a strict diet to lose more weight in addition to their previous weight loss. Amazingly, through their ordeal underground each man lost, on average, eighteen pounds. Each man met the target size in order to fit into the capsule.[67] Victory and praises rang out to God as each man was safely lifted from the depths of the mine, to the waiting arms of loved ones and safety.

Considered a modern-day miracle, these men spent a total of sixty-nine days with death knocking at their door, but each of those days helped to pave the way to their rescue. Although sixty-nine days in those conditions sounds too long, every pound and inch the miners lost secured their ability to fit perfectly into the minuscule capsule. While they appeared to be losing themselves throughout this tragedy, they were actually gaining their freedom. What a powerful object lesson to be learned from the tragedy of these thirty-three men—that their deliverance came from the whittling away of themselves. Even at their darkest hour, God was preparing them for escape. Every hunger pang and dehydrated moment served as stepping stones on the path to liberation.

Likewise, through different and often uncomfortable methods, the Lord will mold and maneuver us to fit the position He needs us to be in. Though it may feel as though the Lord is not intervening, the mighty hands of God are never at rest. As harrowing as a situation may be, at the appointed time and not a moment too soon, the Lord will transport us to a realm of safety, security, and blessings. It is through these experiences that we bear witness to His glory and testify of His goodness in resolving complicated situations, as only the Lord can.

---

67   Kantor, Corinne. "The Chilean Miners Diet." TheFoodCop.com. October 16, 2010. http://www.thefoodcop.com/the-chilean-miners-diet/

Testimonies:

Personal stories of overcoming rejection!

By: Ms. S.L.A.

Rejection as a source of protection. I once thought of this as an unlikely concept. Rejection is a word that is associated with fear and humiliation of the human soul. No one wants to face rejection, but I believe that everyone expects protection at some point in his or her life. So how are the two related? Several experiences with rejection helped me understand that rejection can be a form of protection. The experiences were not easy and caused embarrassment due to lack of understanding. Understanding eventually came with maturity. Maturity brought revelation that when God says no, he does so because He is faithful, loving, and truly desires to protect His children.

What do you do when you seem to find mutual attraction between a Christian single woman and a single Christian male? Your initial introduction begins in the work place and develops into a great working relationship, eventually becoming good friends outside the work environment. There are common interests, similar family background, and you start to meet each other's family. Sounds like a good foundation for exploring a relationship. At least, that's what I thought.

I am a cautious person and pray about everything, so when I knew I was developing feelings for this person, I took initiative and prayed to God. I asked God, if this co-worker approached me, should I accept an invitation to date? Immediately, the answer was no. The answer came so fast that I thought it was the devil trying to keep me from being in a happy and healthy relationship, so I rebuked Satan and continued to pray. No, was the same, strong answer. I asked why. I began to plead my case, telling God that this person was a good man; he was a Christian, and so on and so forth. I stayed in prayer for another moment, hoping for an explanation. God did not respond, and I accepted *no* as the final answer. My acceptance did not keep me from wondering why.

In the months to follow, I became working partners with this person; we were each other's back-up for our caseload. I immediately put up my guard to ensure that I would follow the Lord's direction. As soon as I made a decision to obey God, it seemed that my co-worker and friend began to demonstrate actions that went beyond friendship. Although I mentally questioned his intentions, I remained professional and ignored his behavior. On occasion, I checked myself to determine if my actions were lining up with my decision to obey God. I hoped that it was not my interactions with him that encouraged his behavior. I was determined to be obedient; therefore, I maintained my defenses through all of his flirtatious actions.

After a year in this job, I accepted another position, and the week before I was to leave, God told me to share my feelings with my co-worker. Huh? I was shocked. I asked God why. As far as I was concerned, my co-worker did not need to know what I was feeling. Why would I share this when I could leave with my pride intact? However, the feeling that I was supposed to tell him stayed with me. I was so nervous that I delayed telling him anything for an entire week. On my final day, I transferred my cases to this co-worker. One particular case required us to be in court all day. I had plenty of opportunity to tell him, but I did not say a word. I asked the Lord to forgive me, because I was not going to share my feelings with him. As the workday ended, my coworker and I said our good byes. I remained at the office to finish paperwork. My co-worker left and as the door closed behind him, I breathed a sigh of relief. Again, I asked God to forgive me for being disobedient. No sooner did the prayer leave my mouth than my co-worker opened the door and asked why I let him forget his keys.

Don't tell me that God does not have a sense of humor; better yet, He is the God of the second chance. He is relentless in fulfilling His will. I threw my face into my hands, snickered, and told him that was the Holy Spirit. He asked me what was I talking about, and I asked him how much time he had. This was God giving me a chance to obey.

I quickly shared my feelings and yes, he rejected me, telling me it was not the right time, blah, blah, blah. In my mind I was very immature, thinking, ha, God rejected you first. But that attitude soon dissipated. I became respectful as he began to share his personal story. Although I was embarrassed, I sat and listened to his testimony. I learned that he was a new believer, and although he seemed to be mature, he was in the beginning stages of learning the principles of Christ. I could hear the voice of my pastor, saying, "Don't go snatching men out of the new converts class, let him mature in God first."

I got lost in his story and forgot all that I was supposed to tell him. After two hours of talking, he realized he had locked his keys in his car, and I had to give him a ride home. I thought to myself, are you kidding, God? I still have to face him.

I thought this was some nasty trick; I just wanted to go home. While I drove him, he continued to talk, and I feigned courtesy by giving him the occasional head nod and *mmm-hmm*. As I listened to him, part of me wanted to run and hide because I was drowning in embarrassment, my pride was bruised, and I felt rejected. Having an emotional trial, I lost focus and did not share with him what was most important. I later found out that partial obedience is the same as disobedience.

Fast-forward two years. Although I no longer worked with my friend, occasionally I would speak and meet with other friends who were former colleagues of the same agency. One particular friend asked when I had last spoken with my former back-up partner. It had been a while, and my friend encouraged me to give him a call. The look of concern caused me to probe for more information. Eventually I was told that my friend was soon to be a father. I was stunned. Questions of what, who, and why filled my mind. Ezekiel 33:6-9 came to me, and I had my answer: "But if the watchman sees the sword coming and does not blow the trumpet to warn the people and the sword comes and takes someone's life, that person's life will be taken because of their sin, but I will hold the watchman accountable for their blood."

I was filled with grief, sorrow, and guilt. I wanted to cry, because I did not share the most important information with my friend. I was supposed to tell him that although I considered myself to be strong in the Lord, I had been attracted to him and had to fight temptation, and he needed to be careful with his interactions concerning women, because not all women are spiritually strong and may give into temptation. With this realization, I was crushed; I felt as if I shared in his sin, because I failed to be completely obedient to God. My pride got in the way; "pride goes before destruction, a haughty spirit before a fall."[68] I was prideful, and he fell.

I went home and prayed. How would I call and approach my friend and share my revelation with him? When I called and we met, I shared with him the scripture in Ezekiel and I asked for his forgiveness, because verse 8 is clear—his sin was on my hands because I did not speak to him. He forgave me and said that even sharing this scripture probably would not have deterred from his

---

68   Prov. 16:18 NIV

actions. He shared how the relationship with the mother of his child developed, and I listened to see if the relationship was continuing. He stated that other than co-parenting, the relationship was over. His forgiveness did not alleviate my sense of neglected responsibility. From that moment, I purposed in my heart to be obedient to God at all cost.

Reflecting on the time I prayed to God when I realized I was falling for him gave me great peace about following God's direction even when I don't understand. I can see how rejection in this scenario was God's protection. My flesh wanted something that God did not intend. At the time, I had all of my reasons and rationalizations, but God remained faithful to His nature. I learned that God will keep His children if we want to be kept. I can truly say that I am glad that God said no; I'm glad that I did not follow my flesh. I was not above temptation, and it could have been me having a baby out of wedlock, out of God's plan and intended purpose. I understand that when I chose obedience I chose the covering and covenant of God. Currently, I'm still waiting for a godly relationship with a good Christian man. Will I continue to wait? Certainly! Will I wait until God releases me? Absolutely! What is the lesson? When I made a choice to be obedient by not pursuing a possible relationship with my friend, God's rejection was my protection.

By: Ms. L.D.B.

Like most women, I dreamed of the day I would get married and eventually start a family. My dreams quickly turned into a nightmare when I married someone to whom I was not equally yoked or matched. I had known my ex husband for eight years before getting married. We started as friends and turned into romantic partners. During our friendship, there were a lot of mixed messages and ups and downs. I would continually talk to God and ask Him if this is the man He had chosen for me. The answer was always a resounding "no," yet I continued to pursue my now-ex-husband.

There is definitely truth in the saying that God will give you what you ask, but you need to be prepared for what you receive. I accept my responsibility in choosing this man as my husband, but I do not accept or condone his behavior towards me. My ex-husband was emotionally and psychologically abusive. He would tell me that I was responsible for all of the problems in our relationship and speak negatively about my body. He would say that he was ultimately concerned about my health. He never took responsibility for how he treated me or the impression that I would never be good enough in his eyes. He would blame me when I sought support from my family and friends and even the pastor. He didn't like me "airing our dirty laundry."

Our relationship never had a strong foundation and certainly was not built up in God's love. I couldn't understand why God would deny me love. I experienced constant rejection from my ex-husband. I was confused about whether our relationship would become permanent or fade into the ocean like a sunset. We became engaged and decided to wait to consummate the relationship after our marriage. We waited eight months. I expected that after our union was ordained we would have a healthy physical relationship. Instead, I experienced more rejection. We didn't consummate the marriage until three days after the ceremony. I understand that relationships are about communication, commitment, and compromise, but I was not prepared for the problems that ensued. I questioned whether he loved me and still question whether he is capable of mature, *agape* love.

When I questioned him, he became angry, and rejected me emotionally and physically. Why was he acting this way? This was a rejection of my person. My soul ached for companionship and understanding. I remember crying and calling out to God. God answered me, stating that a man who really loved me would not treat me the way this man was treating me. He again told me that I had a right to give and receive love. I remember that moment being the realization that my marriage was over. I remember feeling rejected and dejected by my husband and by God. I also felt incredible relief from God.

He is a prayer-answering God. In this moment of rejection, He was answering my prayers. Although the loss of my marriage was the deepest, soul-wrenching pain I had experienced up to this point of my existence, I was strengthened. I have never regretted the decision to save myself from any further suffering.

In the past three years, God has continued to sustain me. He has put people in my life who continue to provide me with love and support. He has continued to rebuild and renew me. He continues to show me His capacity for love and my ability to give and receive love. This is not to say that I have not experienced further rejection. I just have a greater capacity to cope with this rejection. I realize that this rejection is truly the fulfillment of His promises for my life. This experience made me stronger and more open to communicating my needs and desires to find a love that is everlasting. The best example of this love is the love God has shown to each of us. I realize my own imperfections are what make me human. Being human means being open to my inherent flaws and being vulnerable. God understands that I will make bad choices and decisions in love. Knowing that His love will ultimately ground me keeps me encouraged.

He loves me when I feel like no one else can find me loveable. He loves me as a father, friend, and lover. There is no other being that can love you in this way. There is no other being that can comfort your soul in this way. His best interest is always *my best interest.*

By Ms. N.P.

I was a young, single mother who had just defeated the odds of dropping out of college when I was able to secure a degree in social work. With prayer and determination, I secured a job at a local hospital performing clinical social work. As time passed, I began to enjoy my job and the profession I love. One day, as I was out and about on my lunch break, I ran into a young man named David who was well known in the community. He was playing minor league baseball and there was no doubt that his skills and talent would soon have him playing baseball in the big league. I was charmed by his bright smile, physique, and mannerisms. It was obvious that he seemed interested in me, so we exchanged telephone numbers. That night, I received a call from David and we spoke on the telephone for hours. It seemed that we had an instant connection, and I just knew that he was my "soul mate."

Our friendship began to blossom and eventually it evolved into a relationship. At the time, David was living with friends, and since I had my own home, I encouraged him to move in with me and my son (who was an infant at the time). My mother was extremely disappointed that David had moved in. My mother saw things in David that I couldn't see, and she kept telling me that I was making a big mistake.

Several months passed and I was head over heels in love with David. He was very interactive with my young son, and he was attentive to my emotional needs. David would travel back and forth out of state during spring training and baseball season to visit with me and my son. And during the time he was away, he would never miss an opportunity to call and say how much he loved us.

As the years passed, David seemed to become more distant and preoccupied (as I thought) with baseball. It seemed to me that his career was more important than his relationship with me and my son. When David returned home after baseball season ended, he would make plans to go out with his friends and exclude me. Some nights, he would come home intoxicated, and there would be some nights when he wouldn't come home at all. This behavior was concerning, and I tried to talk with David about how his "partying" was hurting our relationship. David would apologize, but he continued to repeat the same behaviors.

I loved David so much that I feared losing him and thought about how I could change in order to keep him at home. David's behavior eventually began to affect us financially because he would spend hundreds of dollars partying, and it was questionable if he was seeing other women.

One night I received a call from my cousin, and she informed me that David asked her out on a date and told her that he was interested in her. I was devastated. Later that night, when David returned home, I confronted him and he profusely denied my cousin's accusations. David told me that she was interested in him and tried coming on to him but he stopped her and she became upset. David somehow convinced me that my cousin was trying to break us up since she could not have him.

As baseball season approached, David packed up his belongings and left for training. Prior to leaving, he told me that he loved me and would call once he arrived safely for spring training. David never called. I would try to reach him by phone, but my attempts were unsuccessful. Weeks went by and I never heard from him. I was heartbroken, confused, and devastated. I kept wondering what I did for David to cease talking to me. As the months passed by, I did not hear from or see him until I happened to run into a mutual friend and was told that David visited town frequently to hang out with his buddies. It was at that point that I learned our relationship was in trouble, but I had no clue what I did in order for David to totally reject me.

As the months passed, it was difficult to accept that our relationship was over. It was hard for me to adjust and move on. I had to know why. What did I do to make David fall out of love with me?

David did not have the courage to collect the rest of his belongings from my house, so he sent his younger brother to do so. Out of curiosity, I asked his brother if David was in another relationship, and he just shrugged his shoulders.

As time passed, I became strong enough to deal with the heartache. I was able to get out of bed and go to work instead of calling in sick. I started attending functions with my family and friends instead of making excuses. I began to get out more with my son and engage in fun activities. Life began to look up, and I realized that the person I fell in love with didn't love me; I was only a convenience to him.

One day, my mother called to check on me and voiced that she had some bad news. According to my mother, she learned on the news that the police were looking for someone who allegedly sexually assaulted several women in the neighborhood. Through their investigation, David was arrested for the crimes. Needless to say, I was shocked and saddened about the news. My mother also told me that David was no longer playing professional baseball and that when he was dropped from the roster, he came back home and got involved with the wrong crowd, experimenting with drug use, which resulted in his downfall.

My heart went out to David and his family, and I truly believe that when David's professional career got off to a good start, he got caught up in the "limelight" and lost his direction. As a result, he hurt those near and dear to him, but in the end, he lost everything (baseball career, cars, expensive clothing, etc). David was tried and found guilty of the charges, and he received a life sentence.

It turns out that David's rejection was God protecting me from a life of heartache, embarrassment, and pain. Prior to David's arrest, I forgave him for the hurt and pain he caused me, and I think about him from time to time. I hope that he's atoned for his sins and made amends to those that he hurt.

Initially, David's rejection was difficult to deal with. I wanted revenge because I wanted him to feel the emotional pain he inflicted on me. Then I wished evil on him because it seemed like he was reaping all of the benefits of "stardom," since he was popular in our hometown as a result of playing minor league baseball. As the months passed, I thought life wasn't fair and questioned, "Why do bad things always happen to good people?" It was evident that God wanted to get my attention, and he did so by reminding me that the love I had for David is the same love He has for me, but His love is worth a trillion times more. And His love is unconditional, unfailing, and, better yet, I'm worthy of it.

I realize that God was simply telling me that David was not the guy He appointed for me. As I reflect on my past relationship with David, if I had pursued the relationship, my life would probably be in shambles. Having to deal with the shame and embarrassment of the crimes he committed would be unbearable. Also, having to deal with his "night life" and his infidelity would have instilled insecurities, jealousy, and resentment. My financial status would have been jeopardized, and my reputation certainly would have been damaged.

I've learned through this experience that everything is in God's timing and His plan for our lives. I don't want to lie and say that the hurt of rejection goes away overnight, because it doesn't, but learning how to forgive David set me free from the bondage of hurt feelings and hate.

REPENT

"Ask for Forgiveness"

2 Chronicles 7:14-15 & Ezekiel 18:30

REJOICE

"In all things give thanks!"

1 Thessalonians 5:18

YOUR REJECTION GOD'S PROTECTION

Matthew 21:42, Luke 10:16, & 1 Peter 2:4-10

RECALL

"This I recall to my mind; Therefore, I have hope."

Lamentations 3:20-26

REFOCUS

"Write the vision, make it plain"

Habakkuk 2:2

A UNIQUE BIBLICAL APPROACH
TO UNDERSTANDING ADVERSITY!

YOUR REJECTION GOD'S PROTECTION

CHERYL OSBOURNE CHAVERS
& MICAH CHAVERS

THE REJECTED BOOK COVER!

We were fortunate to have several book cover designs
to choose from and this cover was our second choice.
The front book cover that was selected was designed
from a prototype created by Micah.

CPSIA information can be obtained
at www.ICGtesting.com
Printed in the USA
BVHW03s0218120718
521463BV00001B/11/P